Healthy Meal Prep Cookbook:

1000 Days of Vibrant & Nutritious Recipes to save time and money with tasty grab-and-go choices for breakfast, lunch and dinners you and your family will love

Allison Marvey

Table of Contents

Introduction

Trying to keep up a healthy lifestyle in this fast-paced world that we live in may sometimes seem like an insurmountable challenge. It is not surprising that many of us struggle to put healthy meals at the top of our to-do lists among our hectic schedules given the many demands placed on our time. This is where Healthy Meal Pre comes in to completely transform the method in which we make decisions about our eating habits.

Your road toward a more nourished way of life may be made easier and more enjoyable with the help of Healthy Meal Pre, an all-in-one solution that meets all of your needs. Our goal is to make it easier for you to make decisions that are better for your health while also saving you time and effort that you might put to better use. We think that you may revolutionize your connection with food and open the door to a plethora of advantages that will improve your health as a whole if you adopt the idea of meal preparing and make it a regular part of your life.

You can say goodbye to the anxiety that comes with making hasty choices about meals and the temptation to choose less nutritious alternatives when you use nutritious Meal Prep. Our meticulously compiled library of recipes, which has been designed to accommodate a broad range of dietary preferences and objectives, guarantees that you will always have access to a diverse selection of scrumptious and nutritionally sound meals whenever you need them. Our recipes are designed to accommodate your individual requirements, whether you are adhering to a certain eating regimen, trying to get rid of a few pounds, or just wanting to feed your body.

You may save yourself a lot of time and hassle by planning your meals in advance and devoting a modest amount of time each week to the process of meal preparation. This will allow you to have meals waiting for you that need little effort to prepare or are already prepared. This strategy not only helps you save valuable time during the stressful weekdays, but it also gives you the ability to make more informed decisions about the things you put in your body. You will have a better understanding of your nutritional intake if you control the components and the portion sizes, and you will be able to modify your meals to match your specific objectives if you do this.

At Healthy Meal Pre, we are aware of the fact that adopting a healthy lifestyle is not a path that can be simplified into a single step. Because of this, we give high importance to both variety and adaptability in our recipes. This ensures that you will never get bored with your meals and that you will be able to modify them to fit your preferences. Because of this, our team of nutritionists and culinary specialists toils away day and night to come up with dishes that are not only scrumptious but also beneficial to one's health. We think that eating well should be both pleasurable and practical.

Come along with us on this life-changing adventure to a healthier and happier version of yourself. Discover the flexibility that comes with meal preparation with the help of Healthy Meal Pre, and unleash the myriad advantages that come with placing an emphasis on your own health. You may say goodbye to the daily battle of choosing healthy choices and embrace a lifestyle that supports your objectives, all while appreciating the great tastes of our expertly created meals. This will allow you to say goodbye to the everyday difficulty of making healthy choices. Your journey toward a healthier future may start right now with Healthy Meal Pre.

Meal Prep

Meal prep is an abbreviation for the phrase "meal preparation," which describes the process of organizing and preparing meals ahead of time. It entails setting aside a certain amount of time to prepare and put together meals or components of meals that may be saved and eaten at a later time. In addition to reducing the amount of time and effort required to prepare nutritious meals throughout the week, the primary goal of meal preparation is to encourage individuals to make more healthful decisions about their diets.

Individuals will normally choose recipes, compose a shopping list, and then go out and get the essential products during the meal preparation phase. After that, they devote a focused period of time to preparing the meals, dividing them into individual portions, and placing them in individual servings or containers.

The process of planning, cooking, and portioning meals in advance is referred to as "meal prep." It involves setting aside certain time in order to prepare meals or components of meals that can be saved and eaten at a later time. These meals or components of meals may be eaten whenever they are needed. You may save yourself time and worry during the hectic weekdays by spending a few hours each week in food preparation. This will guarantee that you have meals waiting for you that are either ready to eat or can be easily assembled.

Advantages of meal preparing

Convenience and savings of time are two advantages that come with meal preparation saving.

Preparing meals in advance avoids the need that each day's meals be prepared from scratch. When you're pushed for time, it may be a headache to make selections about what to eat; however, if you plan ahead and prepare your meals, you won't have to worry about that. You will, instead, be provided with pre-portioned meals that can be easily re-heated or constructed in a short amount of time. This will ensure that you always have a wholesome choice available to you.

Options that is better for your health.

When you prepare your meals in advance, you have full discretion over the kinds of foods you eat and the quantities of food you consume at each meal. Because of this, you are able to make conscious decisions about what you eat, which helps to ensure that your meals are well-rounded and in line with the objectives you have set for your diet. Meal preparation helps you maintain a better diet by lowering the amount of dependence you have on bad convenience meals or takeout.

Cost Cuts and Money Saved

Meal preparation might also help you save money. It is possible to generate a shopping list that corresponds with your recipes if you plan your meals in advance. This will help you avoid making rash purchases or wasting food due to a lack of preparation. You may squeeze even more out of your food budget by preparing in larger quantities and serving meals in individual portions.

The Process of Preparing the Meals

Choosing the Recipes

To begin, choose meals that are appropriate for your nutritional tastes, objectives, and any dietary limitations that you may have. Look for recipes that are not only tasty but also provide a good balance of nutrients and a range of options so that you can keep your meals interesting all throughout the week.

Shopping Trips and the Preparation of Ingredients

Make a detailed list of the groceries you need to buy depending on the recipes you've selected. This guarantees that you have all of the required elements available to you. When you get home from the shopping store, spend some time to wash, cut, and otherwise prepare the items so that the process of putting together the dinner may go more quickly.

Cooking and dividing up portions

Cooking and putting together your meals should take place at a designated period of time, such as a few hours on the weekend. Create numerous portions of each dish and divide them into separate containers when you've finished cooking. You may want to keep your meals arranged and make them simple to grab whenever you need them by storing them in little bags or split containers.

The ability to successfully prepare meals is a game-changer for easing the process of eating healthily. You may enjoy the convenience of having healthy meals immediately accessible, save time during the hectic weekdays, and make conscious decisions about what you eat if you spend a little time and work up front. This allows you to enjoy the benefits of having nutritious meals readily available. Embrace meal preparation as a tool to promote your health and unleash the myriad advantages that come with leading a nourished lifestyle.

Importance of lifestyle

In the modern, fast-paced and linked world, the way we live our lives is one of the most important factors in determining our overall health and quality of life. Our physical health, emotional well-being, relationships, and general contentment are all impacted by the choices, habits, and behaviors we participate in on a daily basis, which are collectively referred to as our lifestyle. Understanding the relevance of our way of life gives us the ability to make deliberate choices that contribute to our overall growth and provide us the tools we need to flourish in the face of the pressures and stresses of contemporary life.

Physical Health and Vitality

A healthy lifestyle has a direct influence on our physical health and lays the groundwork for maximum well-being by providing a firm foundation. A healthy lifestyle should include crucial components such as consistent physical activity, good diet, and enough relaxation. The act of participating in physical exercise not only helps our bodies become more robust, but it also improves the health of our cardiovascular systems, our immune systems, our energy levels, and it makes it easier to maintain a healthy weight. These behaviors, in conjunction with a diet that is nutritionally sound, can lower the chance of developing chronic illnesses, extend lifespan, and promote overall vitality.

Psychological and Emotional Health and Well-Being

The decisions we make in our lifestyle have a tremendous impact on both our mental and emotional health. It is helpful to alleviate anxiety, enhance attention, and cultivate a positive mentality by participating in hobbies, practicing mindfulness and meditation, or incorporating stress management strategies into one's daily routine. Recharging our batteries and building up our emotional fortitude may be accomplished by making self-care a priority and establishing and maintaining appropriate boundaries. In addition, improving one's mental health and general level of life satisfaction may be accomplished through cultivating strong connections, finding social support, and developing effective communication skills.

Balance between Work and Personal Life

The successful blending of one's professional life, one's personal life, and one's leisure pursuits is the hallmark of a balanced existence. Achieving a good balance between one's professional life and one's personal life helps avoid burnout, lowers levels of stress, and increases overall productivity as well as job satisfaction. It is possible to increase one's level of happiness and cultivate a feeling of satisfaction in all aspects of life by setting aside time each week to engage in activities such as relaxation, the pursuit of hobbies, and the maintenance of personal connections.

Growth and Learning throughout a Person's Whole Life

Our lives and the world around us may both benefit from adopting a mindset that prioritizes lifelong education and development of the self. Growing our intellectual curiosity, actively seeking out new experiences, and actively participating in lifelong learning via reading, classes, or the development of new skills broadens our views, improves our ability to solve problems, and stimulates our creative thinking. This dedication to improvement not only helps to maintain our mental acuity but also brings about a feeling of personal satisfaction and adds to our sense of purpose.

Eco-Friendly Practices and Conscientiousness of the Environment

The consideration of sustainable practices and being aware of one's impact on the surrounding environment is an essential component of a lifestyle that prioritizes overall wellness. Adopting eco-friendly behaviors, such as decreasing waste, saving energy and water, and making environmentally aware consumer choices, contribute to a healthier world and a brighter future for future generations. These practices include: reducing waste; conserving energy and water; and making environmentally conscious choices as consumers. The demonstration of a commitment to responsible citizenship and a profound regard for the interconnection of all living creatures is provided by the incorporation of sustainable practices into our way of life.

A lifestyle is not only a collection of day-to-day activities; rather, it is an intentional and conscientious route towards achieving overall health and happiness. We may build a life that is full and meaningful for us by placing an emphasis on our physical health, making it a priority to care for our mental and emotional well-being, creating a balance between our professional and personal lives, welcoming personal development, and developing habits that are sustainable. Recognizing the significance of our way of life enables us to make decisions that are beneficial to our health, which in turn paves the way for us to flourish in the contemporary world and lead lives that are rich in energy, purpose, and pleasure.

Meal prep containers

Anyone who engages in the practice of meal planning will find that meal prep containers are an essential piece of equipment. These containers are made to store and carry pre-portioned meals, giving you the ability to remain organized, keep food fresh, and take advantage of the ease of having ready-to-eat or easy-to-assemble meals available to you throughout the week. Let's discuss the advantages of meal prep containers as well as the many kinds that may help you achieve your objectives about healthy eating, shall we?

The Advantages of Using Meal Prep Containers to Control Portion Size

You are able to portion your meals correctly thanks to the availability of meal prep containers in a variety of sizes. This function is essential for supporting weight management or particular dietary objectives, keeping a balanced diet, limiting calorie intake, and maintaining a healthy diet overall.

Food's Freshness and How Long It Will Last

Containers for meal prepping that are of high quality are meant to maintain the food's freshness for longer periods of time. They are generally airtight, leak-proof, and constructed from long-lasting materials, all of which contribute to the preservation of the flavor, texture, and quality of the food you store in them.

Convenience as well as portability are included

You may simply bring your pre-prepared meals to work, school, or with you while you're on the road if you have meal prep containers. Because of their ability to be stacked, they take up less room in your refrigerator or pantry, and the fact that they can tolerate being used in both the microwave and the freezer makes reheating and storing food much simpler.

Simple and Quick Organization

Utilizing containers that are designed for meal preparation makes the process of planning your meals for the week much more manageable. You may label or color-code containers, making it easy to identify certain meals or components and ensuring that you continue to adhere to your meal plan. This will help you remain on track with your diet.

Types of Meal Prep Containers

Containers made of plastic

These containers are not only inexpensive but also lightweight and readily accessible. For the most convenience, look for alternatives that do not contain BPA and are suitable for use in the microwave and dishwasher. Choose containers that have lids that can be securely sealed if you want to avoid leaks and spills.

Containers made of glass

If you want a solution that is better for the environment and more long-lasting, glass meal prep containers are a good choice. They are safe to use in the oven, do not contain any potentially hazardous chemicals, and do an excellent job of keeping heat in. Glass containers are not only visually beautiful but also functional since they may be used as plates for serving.

Containers That Are Divided Into Compartments

These containers come with a number of distinct sections, which enables you to keep various kinds of food products organized inside a single container. Those individuals who want to keep items separate until the time that they are ready to be eaten will find that compartmentalized containers are excellent for their needs.

The use of Mason Jars

Mason jars are multipurpose containers that may be used for preparing food in a variety of ways. They provide a simple means of preserving salads, overnight oats, or foods that have several layers. Mason jars are not only portable and reusable, but they also provide an attractive display for the food you eat.

Containers that can be used to prepare meals are an excellent tool that may make maintaining a balanced diet much easier. You may readily accept meal planning if you make the investment in high-quality containers that provide features like as portion control, food freshness, convenience, and straightforward organizing. Finding the correct containers that fit your requirements can make a major difference in keeping an orderly and comfortable meal preparation routine. This is true whether you go for plastic containers, glass containers, segmented choices, or even reuse mason jars. Put an end to the chaos that is meal planning and say hello to the ease and effectiveness that meal prep containers provide to your healthy way of life.

Breakfast

Overnight Chia Pudding:

Ingredients:

- 2 tablespoons chia seeds
- 1 cup almond milk (or any milk of your choice)
- Sweetener of your choice (honey, maple syrup, or stevia)
- Fresh fruits, nuts, or granola for topping

Directions:

1. First thing in the morning, give the chia pudding a thorough toss to combine the flavors. If the consistency is too thick, you may thin it down by adding a little bit of almond milk.
2. Choose your favorite fresh fruits, nuts, or granola to sprinkle on top of the chia pudding before serving.
3. As a satiating breakfast option, the chia pudding that you make the night before is both creamy and nutrient-dense.

Veggie Egg Muffins:

Ingredients:

- 6 eggs
- 1/2 cup chopped vegetables (bell peppers, spinach, onions, mushrooms, etc.)
- 1/4 cup shredded cheese (cheddar, feta, or your preferred cheese)
- Salt and pepper to taste

Directions:

1. Prepare a muffin tray by greasing it lightly and preheating the oven to 350 degrees Fahrenheit (175 degrees Celsius).
2. In a bowl, beat the eggs with a whisk until they are well combined.
3. Mix in the shredded cheese, grated pepper, and salt after stirring in the chopped veggies.
4. Pour the egg mixture into the muffin tray in a uniform layer, filling each cup to approximately three quarters of its capacity.
5. Bake for 18 to 20 minutes, until the eggs have set and the top is beginning to become golden brown.
6. Take the muffins out of the oven and allow them to cool for a couple of minutes before serving.
7. Egg muffins may be removed from the tin by loosening the edges around them with a knife and then lifting them out.
8. You can either reheat these wonderful vegetarian egg muffins in the oven or store them in the refrigerator for later. They are a convenient alternative for breakfast since they can be rewarmed in the microwave..

Greek Yogurt Parfait:

Ingredients:

- 1 cup Greek yogurt
- 1/2 cup fresh berries (strawberries, blueberries, raspberries)
- 1/4 cup granola
- Honey or maple syrup (optional)

Directions:

1. Put a layer of about a quarter cup of Greek yogurt in the bottom of a glass or jar to get started.
2. On top of the yogurt, arrange a layer of fresh berries in a layer.
3. On top of the berries, strew one tablespoon's worth of granola.
4. Repeat the layering process until all of the ingredients have been used up, then top each finished layer with a dollop of Greek yogurt.
5. Honey or maple syrup, if preferred, may be drizzled over the top to further enhance the sweetness.
6. Breakfast does not get much better than this reviving and satiating Greek Yogurt Parfait, which is packed with protein.

Avocado Toast:

Ingredients:

- 1 ripe avocado
- 2 slices of whole grain bread
- Salt and pepper to taste
- Optional toppings: sliced tomatoes, red pepper flakes, lemon juice, or poached eggs

Directions:

1. Toasted bread with whole grains should have a golden color and a crisp texture.
2. While the bread is being toasted, you should cut the ripe avocado in half, remove the pit, and spoon the flesh from the avocado into a dish.
3. Use a fork to mash the avocado, and then season it with salt and pepper to taste.
4. After the bread has been toasted, put an equal amount of mashed avocado on each piece of it.
5. To serve, top with sliced tomatoes, a sprinkle of red pepper flakes, a squeeze of lemon juice, or a poached egg. All of these toppings are optional.
6. As a revivifying and nutrient-packed breakfast option, serve the avocado toast to your guests.

Smoothie Bowl:

Ingredients:

- 1 ripe banana
- 1 cup frozen berries (strawberries, blueberries, raspberries)
- 1/2 cup almond milk (or any milk of your choice)
- Toppings: sliced fresh fruits, granola, coconut flakes, chia seeds

Directions:

1. Put the ripe banana, frozen berries, and almond milk into a blender and process until smooth.
2. Blend until silky smooth, adding extra milk as necessary to get the desired consistency.
3. The smoothie should be poured into a bowl.
4. Add the toppings that you like the most, such as granola, sliced fresh fruits, coconut flakes, or chia seeds, and serve.
5. As an exciting alternative for breakfast, try out this reviving smoothie bowl that is also loaded with nutrients.

Oatmeal with Toppings:

Ingredients:

- 1/2 cup rolled oats
- 1 cup water or milk
- Pinch of salt
- Toppings: sliced fruits, nuts, seeds, honey or maple syrup

Directions:

1. Put the rolled oats, the water (or milk), and the salt into a small saucepan and stir to mix.
2. Bring the mixture to a boil, and after it has reached a boil, decrease the heat so that it is just simmering.
3. Cook the oats for approximately five minutes, stirring them a few times during that time, until they reach the consistency you want.
4. Take the oatmeal off the stove, and place it in a bowl of your choosing.

5. To serve, top with sliced fruits, nuts, seeds, and honey or maple syrup drizzled over the top.
6. For a hearty and nourishing start to the day, stir up some oats and consume it while it is still warm.

Breakfast Burrito:

Ingredients:

- 2 large eggs
- 2 whole wheat tortillas
- 1/4 cup shredded cheese (cheddar, Monterey Jack, or your preferred cheese)
- 1/4 cup diced vegetables (bell peppers, onions, spinach)
- Salt and pepper to taste
- Salsa or avocado for topping (optional)

Directions:

1. In a bowl, beat the eggs with a whisk until they are well combined. Add little salt and pepper before serving.
2. While it is heating up, gently cover a nonstick pan with cooking spray or oil and place it over medium heat.
3. After the eggs have been whisked, pour them into the frying pan and scramble them for a few minutes until they are fully cooked.
4. To rewarm the tortillas made from whole wheat, use a different pan or the microwave.
5. On each tortilla, spoon one-half of the scrambled eggs and serve.
6. On top of the eggs, sprinkle some grated cheese and chopped bell peppers and onions.
7. To add even more flavor, you might want to top it with salsa or avocado.
8. To construct the shape of a burrito, first fold the edges of the tortilla in toward the center, then wrap it up firmly.
9. As a satiety-inducing and easily transportable morning meal, serve the breakfast tortilla.

Quinoa Breakfast Bowl:

Ingredients:

- 1/2 cup cooked quinoa
- 1/2 cup Greek yogurt
- 1 tablespoon honey or maple syrup
- Fresh berries or sliced fruits
- Chopped nuts or seeds for topping

Directions:

1. In a bowl, combine the cooked quinoa, Greek yogurt, and sweetener of your choice.
2. Stir well to combine the ingredients.
3. Top the quinoa mixture with fresh berries or sliced fruits.
4. Sprinkle with chopped nuts or seeds for added crunch and nutrition.
5. Enjoy this protein-rich and filling quinoa breakfast bowl to start your day right.

Pancakes with Fruit Compote:

Ingredients:

- 1 cup all-purpose flour
- 2 tablespoons sugar
- 1 teaspoon baking powder
- 1/2 teaspoon baking soda
- 1/4 teaspoon salt
- 1 cup buttermilk
- 1 large egg
- 2 tablespoons unsalted butter, melted
- Fruit compote (berries, peaches, or your choice of fruits)
- Maple syrup for serving

Directions:

1. Flour, sugar, baking powder, baking soda, and salt should all be mixed together in a mixing dish using a whisk.
2. Whisk the buttermilk, egg, and melted butter together in a bowl separate from the other ingredients.
3. After pouring the liquid components into the bowl containing the dry ingredients, stir the mixture until it is completely blended. Wait a few minutes before stirring the batter again.
4. Prepare the food on a griddle or pan that does not stick by heating it over medium heat and greasing it gently.
5. For each pancake, pour a quarter cup of the batter onto the hot skillet. After the surface has been cooked until bubbles have formed, turn it and continue to cook it until it is golden brown.
6. Proceed with the remaining batter in the same manner.
7. Warm the fruit compote by heating it in a small saucepan over low heat.
8. Maple syrup should be drizzled over the pancakes after they have been covered with the fruit compote.

Breakfast Quiche:

Ingredients:

- 1 pre-made pie crust
- 4 large eggs
- 1/2 cup milk or cream
- 1 cup chopped vegetables (spinach, mushrooms, onions, bell peppers)
- 1/2 cup shredded cheese (cheddar, Swiss, or your preferred cheese)
- Salt and pepper to taste

Directions:

1. Preheat the oven to 375°F (190°C).
2. Place the pre-made pie crust in a pie dish and set aside.
3. In a bowl, whisk together the eggs, milk or cream, salt, and pepper.
4. Spread the chopped vegetables evenly over the pie crust.
5. Pour the egg mixture over the vegetables.
6. Sprinkle the shredded cheese on top.
7. Bake the quiche in the preheated oven for 30-35 minutes, or until the center is set and the crust is golden brown.
8. Allow the quiche to cool for a few minutes before slicing and serving.

Breakfast Burrito Bowl:

Ingredients:

- 1 cup cooked quinoa or brown rice
- 1/2 cup black beans, drained and rinsed
- 1/2 cup diced tomatoes
- 1/4 cup diced avocado
- 1/4 cup chopped fresh cilantro
- 1/4 cup shredded cheese
- Salsa or hot sauce for topping
- Lime wedges for garnish

Directions:

1. In a bowl, layer the cooked quinoa or brown rice as the base.
2. Top with black beans, diced tomatoes, diced avocado, chopped cilantro, and shredded cheese.
3. Drizzle with salsa or hot sauce according to your preference.
4. Garnish with lime wedges.
5. Mix the ingredients together just before eating or enjoy them layered.
6. This breakfast burrito bowl is customizable and can be modified to include your favorite toppings and proteins.

Egg and Vegetable Wrap:

Ingredients:

- 2 large eggs
- 1 whole wheat tortilla
- 1/4 cup diced vegetables (bell peppers, onions, spinach)
- Salt and pepper to taste
- Optional: Sliced avocado, hot sauce, or salsa for topping

Directions:

1. Place the eggs in a small bowl and use a whisk to thoroughly beat them. Add little salt and pepper before serving.
2. Place a non-stick skillet over medium heat, and using cooking spray or oil, gently cover the surface of the pan.
3. Add the diced veggies to the pan and cook them over medium heat until they are cooked.
4. Add the eggs that have been beaten to the veggies already in the skillet. Cook the eggs, giving them the odd toss, until they are scrambled and cooked all the way through.
5. Heat the tortilla made with whole wheat in a different pan or in the microwave.
7. Atop the tortilla, arrange the scrambled eggs and the sliced veggies.

8. For additional flavor, if desired, top with sliced avocado, spicy sauce, or salsa. This step is optional.
9. Create a wrap by firmly rolling up the tortilla and tucking in the edges of the tortilla as you go.
10. For a filling breakfast that you can take with you, try the egg and veggie wrap that is filled with nutrients and protein.

Green Smoothie

Ingredients:

- 1 ripe banana
- 1 cup fresh spinach or kale leaves
- 1/2 cup frozen pineapple chunks
- 1/2 cup almond milk or coconut water
- Optional: Chia seeds or flaxseeds for added nutrition

Directions:

1. In a blender, combine the ripe banana, fresh spinach or kale, frozen pineapple chunks, and almond milk or coconut water.
2. Blend until smooth and creamy, adding more liquid if needed.
3. Optional: Add a tablespoon of chia seeds or flaxseeds for extra fiber and omega-3 fatty acids.
4. Pour the green smoothie into a glass and enjoy this refreshing and nutrient-rich breakfast.

Cottage Cheese and Fruit Bowl:

Ingredients:

- 1/2 cup cottage cheese
- 1/2 cup fresh berries (strawberries, blueberries, raspberries)
- 1/4 cup sliced peaches or any fruit of your choice
- 1 tablespoon honey or maple syrup
- Optional: Sprinkle of granola or chopped nuts for crunch

Directions:

1. Put the cottage cheese in the bottom of a bowl to use as a basis.
2. Fresh berries, sliced peaches, and any other kinds of fruit that you like should go on top.
3. To add a touch of sweetness, drizzle with honey or maple syrup.
4. Optional: Granola or chopped almonds may be sprinkled on top for an additional textural and crunching element.
5. You may choose to combine the ingredients shortly before eating, or you can enjoy them in layered form.
6. A nutritious start to the day begins with this dish of cottage cheese and fruit, which offers a good combination of protein, fiber, and vitamins.

Breakfast Quinoa Muffins:

Ingredients:

- 1 cup cooked quinoa
- 1/2 cup whole wheat flour
- 1/2 cup oats
- 1/4 cup honey or maple syrup
- 1/4 cup unsweetened applesauce
- 1/4 cup almond milk or any milk of your choice
- 1 teaspoon baking powder
- 1/2 teaspoon cinnamon
- 1/4 teaspoon salt
- 1/4 cup dried fruits (raisins, cranberries) or chopped nuts (optional)

Directions:

1. Preheat the oven to 350°F (175°C) and line a muffin tin with paper liners or grease it lightly.
2. In a large bowl, combine the cooked quinoa, whole wheat flour, oats, baking powder, cinnamon, and salt.
3. In a separate bowl, whisk together the honey or maple syrup, unsweetened applesauce, and almond milk until well combined.
4. Pour the wet ingredients into the dry ingredients and stir until just combined.
5. If desired, fold in dried fruits or chopped nuts.
6. Spoon the batter into the prepared muffin tin, filling each cup about 3/4 full.
7. Bake for 18-20 minutes or until a toothpick inserted into the center comes out clean.
8. Allow the muffins to cool in the tin for a few minutes, then transfer them to a wire rack to cool completely.
9. Enjoy these nutritious Breakfast Quinoa Muffins as a grab-and-go option for a healthy breakfast.

Grains and beans

Quinoa and Black Bean Salad:

Ingredients:

- 1 cup quinoa
- 1 can black beans, drained and rinsed
- 1 cup diced tomatoes
- 1 cup diced cucumbers
- 1/4 cup chopped cilantro
- Juice of 1 lime

Directions:

1. Cook the quinoa in accordance with the directions on the box, and then let it to cool.
2. Incorporate the cooked quinoa, black beans, diced tomatoes, diced cucumbers, chopped cilantro, and lime juice in a large bowl and stir to incorporate. After thoroughly combining, serve.

Chickpea Curry with Brown Rice:

Ingredients:

- 1 cup cooked brown rice
- 1 can chickpeas, drained
- 1 onion, chopped
- 2 cloves garlic, minced
- 1-inch piece of ginger, grated
- 1 tablespoon curry powder
- 1 teaspoon cumin
- 1/2 teaspoon turmeric
- 1/2 teaspoon chili powder
- 1 can coconut milk
- Salt and pepper to taste

Directions:

1. Sauté the onion, garlic, and ginger in a large pan until the onion, garlic, and ginger release their aroma.
2. Curry powder, cumin, turmeric, and chili powder should all be added now. Stir thoroughly.
3. The chickpeas and the coconut milk should be added. Simmer for 10-15 minutes.
4. Salt and pepper may be added to taste as a seasoning. The curry should be served over brown rice that has been prepared.

Mexican Quinoa Bowl:

Ingredients:

- 1 cup cooked quinoa
- 1 can black beans, drained and rinsed
- 1 cup corn kernels
- 1 avocado, diced
- 1 cup diced tomatoes
- 1/4 cup chopped cilantro
- Juice of 1 lime
- 2 tablespoons olive oil
- 1/2 teaspoon cumin
- Salt and pepper to taste

Directions:

1. Mix together in a dish the quinoa that has been cooked, the black beans, the corn kernels, the avocado that has been diced, the tomatoes that have been diced, and the chopped cilantro.
2. To prepare the dressing, put the lime juice, olive oil, cumin, salt, and pepper into a small dish and mix all of the ingredients together.
3. After pouring the dressing over the quinoa mixture, give it a thorough tossing to integrate everything. Serve.

Lentil Soup:

Ingredients:

- 1 cup dried lentils
- 1 onion, diced
- 2 carrots, diced
- 2 celery stalks, diced
- 3 cloves garlic, minced
- 4 cups vegetable broth
- 1 can diced tomatoes
- 1 teaspoon dried thyme
- 1 teaspoon dried oregano
- Salt and pepper to taste

Directions:

1. After being washed in ice-cold water, the lentils should be placed aside.
2. Sauté the onion, carrots, celery, and garlic in a large saucepan over medium heat until the vegetables are tender.
3. Next, stir in the diced tomatoes, thyme, and oregano, followed by the lentils and vegetable broth. Bring the liquid to a boil.
4. Turn the heat down to low and cook the lentils for approximately half an hour, or until they are soft.
5. Salt and pepper may be added to taste as a seasoning. To be served hot.

Black Bean and Sweet Potato Tacos:

Ingredients:

- 2 cups diced sweet potatoes
- 1 can black beans, drained and rinsed
- 1 teaspoon cumin
- 1/2 teaspoon garlic powder
- 1/2 teaspoon chili powder
- 8 small tortillas
- Diced tomatoes, sliced avocado, and chopped cilantro for toppings

Directions:

1. Turn the temperature on the oven to 400 degrees Fahrenheit (200 degrees Celsius).
2. Spread the diced sweet potatoes out on a baking sheet and toss them with olive oil before placing the sheet in the oven.
3. Roast the sweet potatoes in their diced form for around 20 to 25 minutes, or until they are soft.
4. Combine the black beans, cumin, garlic powder, and chili powder in a small bowl and mash them together.
5. To reheat the tortillas, you may use either a skillet or the microwave.
6. Onto the tortillas, spread the black bean puree that has been crushed.
7. To finish, sprinkle the dish with chopped cilantro, diced tomatoes, sliced avocado, and roasted sweet potatoes.
8. After folding the tortillas, the tacos should be served.

Quinoa Stuffed Bell Peppers:

Ingredients:

- 4 bell peppers
- 1 cup cooked quinoa
- 1 can black beans, drained and rinsed
- 1 cup diced tomatoes
- 1/2 cup diced onions
- 1/2 cup corn kernels
- 1 teaspoon cumin
- 1/2 teaspoon chili powder
- Salt and pepper to taste
- Grated cheese (optional)

Directions:

1. Turn the temperature on the oven to 375 degrees Fahrenheit (190 degrees Celsius).
2. Remove the seeds and membranes from the bell peppers, then cut off the tops of the peppers.
3. Combine the following ingredients in a bowl: cooked quinoa, black beans, diced tomatoes, chopped onions, corn kernels, cumin, chili powder, salt, and pepper. Mix well.
4. Place the quinoa-filled bell peppers on a baking dish and bake them. Stuff the bell peppers with the quinoa mixture.
5. On top of the filled peppers, you may add some grated cheese if you'd want to.
6. Bake at 400 degrees for approximately 25 to 30 minutes, or until the peppers are soft and the mixture is completely cooked.

Mediterranean Chickpea Salad:

Ingredients:

- 1 can chickpeas, drained and rinsed
- 1 cup diced cucumbers
- 1 cup diced tomatoes
- 1/2 cup diced red onions
- 1/4 cup chopped parsley
- 1/4 cup chopped mint
- Juice of 1 lemon
- 2 tablespoons olive oil
- Salt and pepper to taste

Directions:

1. Combine all of the ingredients for the salad, including the chickpeas, cucumbers, tomatoes, red onions, parsley, and mint, in a large bowl.
2. To prepare the dressing, put the lemon juice, olive oil, salt, and pepper in a small bowl and mix them together with a whisk.
3. After pouring the dressing over the salad, give it a good spin to mix everything. Refrigerate for at least 30 minutes before serving.

Black Bean Quinoa Burgers:

Ingredients:

- 1 can black beans, drained and rinsed
- 1 cup cooked quinoa
- 1/2 cup breadcrumbs
- 1/4 cup diced onions
- 2 cloves garlic, minced
- 1 teaspoon cumin
- 1/2 teaspoon chili powder
- Salt and pepper to taste
- Burger buns and desired toppings

Directions:

1. To get a chunky consistency, mash the black beans in a bowl using a fork or a potato masher.
2. The mashed black beans should have quinoa that has been cooked, breadcrumbs, onions, garlic, cumin, chili powder, salt, and pepper added to it. Combine thoroughly.
3. Make burger patties out of the mixture, forming them to the appropriate size.
4. Cook the patties for about four to five minutes on each side in a pan that has oil heated over medium heat until they are golden brown.
5. Buns should be used for serving the black bean quinoa burgers, and your preferred toppings should be used.

Spinach and White Bean Soup:

Ingredients:

- 1 tablespoon olive oil
- 1 onion, chopped
- 2 cloves garlic, minced
- 4 cups vegetable broth
- 1 can white beans, drained and rinsed
- 4 cups fresh spinach leaves
- 1 teaspoon dried thyme
- Salt and pepper to taste

Directions:

1. To get a chunky consistency, mash the black beans in a bowl using a fork or a potato masher.
2. The mashed black beans should have quinoa that has been cooked, breadcrumbs, onions, garlic, cumin, chili powder, salt, and pepper added to it. Combine thoroughly.
3. Make burger patties out of the mixture, forming them to the appropriate size.
4. Cook the patties for about four to five minutes on each side in a pan that has oil heated over medium heat until they are golden brown.
5. Buns should be used for serving the black bean quinoa burgers, and your preferred toppings should be used.

Brown Rice and Lentil Stir-Fry:

Ingredients:

- 1 cup cooked brown rice
- 1 cup cooked lentils
- 1 tablespoon sesame oil
- 1 onion, sliced
- 1 carrot, julienned
- 1 bell pepper, sliced
- 1 cup broccoli florets
- 2 cloves garlic, minced
- 2 tablespoons soy sauce
- 1 tablespoon rice vinegar
- 1 tablespoon honey (or alternative sweetener)
- 1 teaspoon grated ginger
- Salt and pepper to taste
- Optional toppings: sliced green onions, sesame seeds

Directions:

1. In a large skillet or wok, bring the sesame oil to a medium temperature.
2. To the pan, add broccoli florets, sliced onion, carrots that have been julienned, and bell peppers that have been sliced. Stir-fry the veggies for a few minutes, or until they begin to get more tender.
3. Mix in the garlic that has been minced, soy sauce, rice vinegar, honey, ginger that has been grated, salt, and pepper. Continue to stir-fry for one more minute.
4. Put brown rice and lentils that have been cooked into the pan. Stir fry everything until it is completely incorporated and has reached the desired temperature.
5. Serve the stir-fry while it is still hot, and if you want, you may top it with chopped green onions and sesame seeds before serving.

Moroccan Chickpea and Couscous Salad:

Ingredients:

- 1 cup couscous
- 1 can chickpeas, drained and rinsed
- 1 cup diced cucumbers
- 1 cup diced tomatoes
- 1/2 cup chopped fresh parsley
- 1/4 cup chopped fresh mint
- Juice of 1 lemon
- 2 tablespoons olive oil
- 1 teaspoon ground cumin
- 1/2 teaspoon ground cinnamon
- Salt and pepper to taste

Directions:

1. Prepare the couscous according to the package instructions and let it cool.
2. In a large bowl, combine cooked couscous, chickpeas, cucumbers, tomatoes, parsley, and mint.
3. In a small bowl, whisk together lemon juice, olive oil, cumin, cinnamon, salt, and pepper to make the dressing.
4. Drizzle the dressing over the couscous mixture and toss well to combine. Refrigerate for at least 30 minutes before serving.

Black Bean and Quinoa Stuffed Zucchini:

Ingredients:

- 4 medium zucchini
- 1 cup cooked quinoa
- 1 can black beans, drained and rinsed
- 1/2 cup diced bell peppers
- 1/2 cup corn kernels
- 1/2 cup diced tomatoes
- 1/4 cup chopped cilantro
- 1 teaspoon cumin
- 1/2 teaspoon chili powder
- Salt and pepper to taste
- Grated cheese (optional)

Directions:

1. Turn the temperature on the oven to 375 degrees Fahrenheit (190 degrees Celsius).
2. After cutting the zucchini in half lengthwise, scrape the flesh out of each half, leaving behind a shell that has been hollowed out.
3. Cooked quinoa, black beans, diced bell peppers, corn kernels, diced tomatoes, chopped cilantro, cumin, chili powder, salt, and pepper are combined in a dish and mixed together.
4. Put the quinoa mixture into the zucchini shells that have been hollowed out, and set the zucchini shells on a baking sheet.
5. You may top the filled zucchini with grated cheese if you want, but it's not required.
6. Bake for about 20 to 25 minutes, or until the zucchini is soft and the mixture is cooked all the way through.

Barley and Bean Salad:

Ingredients:

- 1 cup cooked barley
- 1 can kidney beans, drained and rinsed
- 1 cup halved cherry tomatoes
- 1/2 cup diced red onions
- 1/4 cup chopped fresh parsley
- Juice of 1 lemon
- 2 tablespoons olive oil
- 1 teaspoon Dijon mustard
- Salt and pepper to taste

Directions:

1. In a large bowl, combine cooked barley, kidney beans, cherry tomatoes, red onions, and parsley.
2. In a small bowl, whisk together lemon juice, olive oil, Dijon mustard, salt, and pepper to make the dressing.
3. Pour the dressing over the salad and toss well to combine. Refrigerate for at least 30 minutes before serving.

Red Lentil and Vegetable Curry:

Ingredients:

- 1 cup red lentils
- 1 onion, chopped
- 2 cloves garlic, minced
- 1-inch piece of ginger, grated
- 1 can coconut milk
- 1 cup diced bell peppers
- 1 cup diced zucchini
- 1 cup diced eggplant
- 1 tablespoon curry powder
- 1 teaspoon ground cumin
- 1/2 teaspoon ground turmeric
- Salt and pepper to taste
- Fresh cilantro for garnish

Directions:

1. After being washed in ice-cold water, the red lentils should be placed aside.
2. Cook the chopped onion, minced garlic, and grated ginger in a large saucepan over medium heat until the onion, garlic, and ginger release their aroma.
3. Place in the saucepan the chopped bell peppers, zucchini, eggplant, curry powder, cumin, turmeric, salt, and pepper. Also add the red lentils. Stir thoroughly.
4. The mixture should be brought to a boil, after which the heat should be reduced and it should be allowed to simmer for around 20–25 minutes, or until the lentils and veggies are cooked.
5. Before serving, garnish with freshly chopped cilantro. Rice or naan bread should be served with the dish.

Durable salads

Greek Salad

Ingredients:

- 2 cups chopped romaine lettuce
- 1 cup diced cucumbers
- 1 cup halved cherry tomatoes
- 1/2 cup diced red onions
- 1/4 cup sliced Kalamata olives
- 1/4 cup crumbled feta cheese
- 2 tablespoons extra virgin olive oil
- Juice of 1 lemon
- Salt and pepper to taste

Directions:

1. Put the romaine lettuce, cucumbers, cherry tomatoes, red onions, Kalamata olives, and feta cheese into a big bowl and mix everything together.
2. Olive oil and lemon juice should be drizzled over the fish.
3. Add little salt and pepper before serving.
4. To incorporate everything, give it a good toss, then serve.

Quinoa and Chickpea Salad

Ingredients:

- 1 cup cooked quinoa
- 1 can chickpeas, drained and rinsed
- 1 cup diced cucumbers
- 1 cup diced tomatoes
- 1/4 cup chopped fresh parsley
- 2 tablespoons lemon juice
- 2 tablespoons extra virgin olive oil
- Salt and pepper to taste

Directions:

1. Mix the cooked quinoa, chickpeas, cucumbers, tomatoes, and chopped parsley together in a large bowl.
2. To prepare the dressing, put the lemon juice, olive oil, salt, and pepper in a small bowl and mix them together with a whisk.
3. After drizzling the dressing over the salad, toss it well to mix everything.
4. You may serve the dish either cold or at room temperature. Mix the cooked quinoa, chickpeas, cucumbers, tomatoes, and chopped parsley together in a large bowl.
5. To prepare the dressing, put the lemon juice, olive oil, salt, and pepper in a small bowl and mix them together with a whisk.
6. After drizzling the dressing over the salad, toss it well to mix everything.
7. You may serve the dish either cold or at room temperature.

Asian Noodle Salad

Ingredients:

- 8 oz soba noodles, cooked and cooled
- 1 cup shredded cabbage
- 1 cup julienned carrots
- 1/2 cup sliced bell peppers
- 1/4 cup chopped green onions
- 1/4 cup chopped cilantro
- 2 tablespoons sesame oil
- 2 tablespoons soy sauce
- 1 tablespoon rice vinegar
- 1 tablespoon honey (or alternative sweetener)
- 1 teaspoon grated ginger
- Sesame seeds for garnish

Directions:

1. Mix together in a large bowl the soba noodles that have been cooked, shredded cabbage, carrots, bell peppers, green onions, and cilantro.
2. The dressing may be made by combining sesame oil, soy sauce, rice vinegar, honey, and grated ginger in a small bowl and whisking the ingredients together.
3. After pouring the dressing over the salad, give it a good spin to mix everything.
4. Before serving, sprinkle some toasted sesame seeds on top.

Caprese Quinoa Salad

Ingredients:

- 1 cup cooked quinoa
- 1 cup cherry tomatoes, halved
- 1 cup mozzarella balls (bocconcini), halved
- 1/4 cup chopped fresh basil
- 2 tablespoons balsamic vinegar
- 2 tablespoons extra virgin olive oil
- Salt and pepper to taste

Directions:

1. Combine the quinoa that has been cooked, cherry tomatoes, mozzarella balls, and fresh basil in a big bowl.
2. To prepare the dressing, put the balsamic vinegar, olive oil, salt, and pepper into a small bowl and mix all of the ingredients together.
3. After drizzling the dressing over the salad, toss it well to mix everything.
4. You may serve the dish either cold or at room temperature.

Mexican Quinoa Salad

Ingredients:

- 1 cup cooked quinoa
- 1 can black beans, drained and rinsed
- 1 cup diced tomatoes
- 1/2 cup diced red onions
- 1/2 cup corn kernels
- 1/4 cup chopped fresh cilantro
- Juice of 1 lime
- 2 tablespoons olive oil
- 1 teaspoon cumin
- Salt and pepper to taste
- Optional toppings: diced avocado, sliced jalapeños, crushed tortilla chips

Directions:

1. Mix together in a large bowl the quinoa that has been cooked, black beans, tomatoes, red onions, corn kernels, and cilantro.
2. To prepare the dressing, put the lime juice, olive oil, cumin, salt, and pepper into a small dish and mix all of the ingredients together.
3. After drizzling the dressing over the salad, toss it well to mix everything.
4. You may serve the dish either cold or at room temperature.
5. If you choose, you may sprinkle the top with crumbled tortilla chips, chopped avocado, and sliced jalapenos.

Mediterranean Chickpea Salad

Ingredients:

- 1 can chickpeas, drained and rinsed
- 1 cup diced cucumbers
- 1 cup halved cherry tomatoes
- 1/2 cup diced red onions
- 1/4 cup sliced Kalamata olives
- 1/4 cup crumbled feta cheese
- 2 tablespoons chopped fresh parsley
- 2 tablespoons lemon juice
- 2 tablespoons extra virgin olive oil
- Salt and pepper to taste

Directions:

1. Chickpeas, cucumbers, cherry tomatoes, red onions, Kalamata olives, and parsley should be mixed together in a big bowl before being topped with feta cheese.
2. To prepare the dressing, put the lemon juice, olive oil, salt, and pepper in a small bowl and mix them together with a whisk.
3. After drizzling the dressing over the salad, toss it well to mix everything.
4. You may serve the dish either cold or at room temperature.

Kale and Quinoa Salad

Ingredients:

- 4 cups chopped kale leaves
- 1 cup cooked quinoa
- 1 cup diced apples
- 1/2 cup dried cranberries
- 1/4 cup sliced almonds
- 2 tablespoons lemon juice
- 2 tablespoons extra virgin olive oil
- 1 tablespoon honey (or alternative sweetener)
- Salt and pepper to taste

Directions:

1. Combine kale that has been chopped, quinoa that has been cooked, apple that has been diced, cranberries that have been dried, and almonds that have been sliced in a big bowl.
2. To prepare the dressing, put the lemon juice, olive oil, honey, salt, and pepper into a small dish and mix all of the ingredients together.
3. After drizzling the dressing over the salad, toss it well to mix everything.
4. Give the salad a few minutes to settle so that the kale may have a chance to relax and soften.
5. You may serve the dish either cold or at room temperature.

Tuna and White Bean Salad

Ingredients:

- 2 cans tuna, drained
- 1 can white beans, drained and rinsed
- 1 cup diced celery
- 1/2 cup diced red onions
- 1/4 cup chopped fresh parsley
- 2 tablespoons lemon juice
- 2 tablespoons extra virgin olive oil
- Salt and pepper to taste

Directions:

1. In a large bowl, combine tuna, white beans, celery, red onions, and parsley.
2. In a small bowl, whisk together lemon juice, olive oil, salt, and pepper to make the dressing.
3. Drizzle the dressing over the salad and toss well to combine.
4. Serve chilled or at room temperature.
5. This salad can be enjoyed as a sandwich filling or on a bed of mixed greens.

Beet and Goat Cheese Salad

Ingredients:

- 4 cups mixed salad greens
- 2 medium beets, roasted, peeled, and sliced
- 1/2 cup crumbled goat cheese
- 1/4 cup chopped walnuts
- 2 tablespoons balsamic vinegar
- 2 tablespoons extra virgin olive oil
- Salt and pepper to taste

Directions:

1. Combined salad greens, roasted beets, crumbled goat cheese, and chopped walnuts should be combined together in a big bowl.
2. To prepare the dressing, put the balsamic vinegar, olive oil, salt, and pepper into a small bowl and mix all of the ingredients together.
3. After drizzling the dressing over the salad, toss it well to mix everything.
4. Serve immediately.

Spinach and Strawberry Salad

Ingredients:

- 4 cups baby spinach leaves
- 1 cup sliced strawberries
- 1/4 cup crumbled feta cheese
- 1/4 cup sliced almonds
- 2 tablespoons balsamic vinegar
- 2 tablespoons extra virgin olive oil
- 1 tablespoon honey (or alternative sweetener)
- Salt and pepper to taste

Directions:

1. Baby spinach leaves, sliced strawberries, crumbled feta cheese, and sliced almonds should be mixed together in a big bowl before serving.

2. To create the dressing, put the balsamic vinegar, olive oil, honey, salt, and pepper into a small bowl and mix all of the ingredients together.
3. After drizzling the dressing over the salad, toss it well to mix everything.
4. Immediately serve after cooking.

Quinoa and Roasted Vegetable Salad

Ingredients:

- 1 cup cooked quinoa
- 1 cup roasted vegetables (such as bell peppers, zucchini, and eggplant)
- 1/4 cup crumbled goat cheese
- 2 tablespoons chopped fresh basil
- 2 tablespoons lemon juice
- 2 tablespoons extra virgin olive oil
- Salt and pepper to taste

Directions:

1. Mix together cooked quinoa, veggies that have been roasted, goat cheese that has been crumbled, and fresh basil that has been chopped in a big bowl.
2. To prepare the dressing, put the lemon juice, olive oil, salt, and pepper in a small bowl and mix them together with a whisk.
3. After drizzling the dressing over the salad, toss it well to mix everything.
4. You may serve the dish either cold or at room temperature.

Cobb Salad

Ingredients:

- 4 cups chopped romaine lettuce
- 2 hard-boiled eggs, sliced
- 1 cup diced cooked chicken breast
- 1/2 cup diced tomatoes
- 1/2 cup diced cucumbers
- 1/4 cup crumbled blue cheese
- 2 slices cooked bacon, crumbled
- 2 tablespoons ranch dressing

Directions:

1. Mix together cooked quinoa, veggies that have been roasted, goat cheese that has been crumbled, and fresh basil that has been chopped in a big bowl.
2. To prepare the dressing, put the lemon juice, olive oil, salt, and pepper in a small bowl and mix them together with a whisk.
3. After drizzling the dressing over the salad, toss it well to mix everything.
4. You may serve the dish either cold or at room temperature.

Mediterranean Orzo Salad

Ingredients:

- 1 cup cooked orzo pasta
- 1/2 cup diced cucumber
- 1/2 cup halved cherry tomatoes
- 1/4 cup diced red onions
- 1/4 cup sliced Kalamata olives
- 1/4 cup crumbled feta cheese
- 2 tablespoons chopped fresh parsley
- 2 tablespoons lemon juice
- 2 tablespoons extra virgin olive oil
- Salt and pepper to taste

Directions:

1. Orzo pasta that has been cooked, cucumber that has been chopped, cherry tomatoes, red onions, Kalamata olives, feta cheese, and parsley should be mixed together in a big bowl.
2. To prepare the dressing, put the lemon juice, olive oil, salt, and pepper in a small bowl and mix them together with a whisk.
3. After drizzling the dressing over the salad, toss it well to mix everything.
4. You may serve the dish either cold or at room temperature.

Southwestern Black Bean Salad

Ingredients

- 1 can black beans, drained and rinsed
- 1 cup diced tomatoes
- 1/2 cup diced red
- Onions
- 1/2 cup corn kernels
- 1/4 cup chopped fresh cilantro
- 2 tablespoons lime juice
- 2 tablespoons olive oil
- 1 teaspoon cumin
- 1/2 teaspoon chili powder
- Salt and pepper to taste
- Optional toppings: diced avocado, sliced jalapeños, crushed tortilla chips

Directions:

1. In a large bowl, combine black beans, tomatoes, red onions, corn kernels, and cilantro.
2. In a small bowl, whisk together lime juice, olive oil, cumin, chili powder, salt, and pepper to make the dressing.
3. Drizzle the dressing over the salad and toss well to combine.
4. Serve chilled or at room temperature.
5. If desired, top with diced avocado, sliced jalapeños, and crushed tortilla chips.

Quinoa and Kale Salad

Ingredients:

- 1 cup cooked quinoa
- 4 cups chopped kale leaves
- 1 cup diced cucumbers
- 1/2 cup diced bell peppers
- 1/4 cup sliced almonds
- 2 tablespoons lemon juice
- 2 tablespoons extra virgin olive oil
- 1 tablespoon Dijon mustard
- Salt and pepper to taste

Directions:

1. Mix together in a large bowl the quinoa that has been cooked, the chopped kale, the cucumbers, the bell peppers, and the sliced almonds.
2. To prepare the dressing, put some lemon juice, olive oil, Dijon mustard, some salt, and some pepper in a small bowl and mix all of those ingredients together.
3. After drizzling the dressing over the salad, toss it well to mix everything.
4. Give the salad a few minutes to settle so that the kale may have a chance to relax and soften.
5. You may serve the dish either cold or at room temperature.

Fish and sea food

Tilapia with Red Onion and Avocado

Ingredients:

- 4 tilapia fillets
- 1 red onion, thinly sliced
- 1 avocado, sliced
- Juice of 1 lime
- Salt and pepper to taste
- Fresh cilantro for garnish

Directions:

1. Turn the temperature on the oven to 400 degrees Fahrenheit (200 degrees Celsius).
2. After adding salt and pepper to taste, arrange the tilapia fillets in a single layer on a baking sheet.
3. Place a few slices of red onion on top of each fillet, then sprinkle with lime juice.
4. Bake the fish in an oven that has been warmed for 12 to 15 minutes, or until it reaches an internal temperature of 145 degrees Fahrenheit.
5. Take the dish out of the oven and garnish it with sliced avocado and fresh cilantro.
6. To be served hot.

Grilled Fish on Lemons

Ingredients:

- 4 fish fillets (such as salmon, halibut, or snapper)
- 2 lemons, sliced
- 2 tablespoons olive oil
- Salt and pepper to taste
- Fresh dill for garnish

Directions:

1. Prepare the grill for cooking over a medium heat.
2. Arrange lemon slices in a single layer on the grate of the grill.
3. Salt, pepper, and olive oil are the seasonings that should be used on the fish fillets.
4. On top of the lemon slices, lay the fish fillets in a single layer.
5. Cook the fish on the grill for four to six minutes each side, or until it is fully done.
6. Take the food off the grill, and sprinkle it with some fresh dill.
7. To be served hot.

Sheet Pan Fish

Ingredients:

- 4 white fish fillets (such as cod or haddock)
- 1 pound baby potatoes, halved
- 1 cup cherry tomatoes
- 1 tablespoon olive oil
- 2 cloves garlic, minced
- 1 teaspoon dried thyme
- Salt and pepper to taste
- Lemon wedges for serving

Directions:

1. Put the oven on to a temperature of 425 degrees Fahrenheit (220 degrees Celsius).
2. Baby potatoes and cherry tomatoes should be halved and placed in a big bowl. Halved baby potatoes and cherry tomatoes should be tossed with olive oil, minced garlic, dried thyme, salt, and pepper.
3. Prepare a baking sheet for the potatoes and tomatoes that have been seasoned.

4. After adding salt and pepper to taste, arrange the fish fillets on top of the veggies in the baking dish.
5. Bake in an oven that has been warmed for about fifteen to twenty minutes, or until the fish is fully cooked and the potatoes are soft.
6. Serve piping hot with lemon slices on the side.

Fish Sticks with a Crispy Polenta Coating

Ingredients:

- 1 pound white fish fillets (such as cod or tilapia), cut into strips
- 1 cup polenta (cornmeal)
- 1 teaspoon paprika
- 1/2 teaspoon garlic powder
- 1/2 teaspoon dried oregano
- Salt and pepper to taste
- 2 eggs, beaten
- Cooking spray

Directions:

1. Prepare a baking sheet by lining it with parchment paper and preheating the oven to 425 degrees Fahrenheit (220 degrees Celsius).
2. Mix together the polenta, paprika, garlic powder, dried oregano, salt, and pepper in a plate that is rather shallow.
3. After being coated with the polenta mixture, each fish strip should be dipped in beaten eggs first.
4. Put the fish strips that have been coated on the baking sheet that has been prepared.
5. Spray some cooking spray on top of the fish sticks so that it lightly coats them.
6. Bake for 12 to 15 minutes in an oven that has been preheated, or until the fish is completely cooked through and the coating is crisp.
7. Serve piping hot with the dipping sauce of your choice.

Salmon in a Skillet

Ingredients:

- 4 salmon fillets
- 1 tablespoon olive oil
- Juice of 1 lemon
- 2 cloves garlic, minced
- 1 teaspoon dried dill
- Salt and pepper to taste

Directions:

1. In a pan, bring the olive oil to a temperature of medium heat.
2. Salt and pepper should be used to season the salmon fillets.
3. Put the fillets on the pan so that the skin side is facing down.
4. Mix the lemon juice, garlic that has been minced, and dill that has been dried together in a small bowl.
5. The salmon should be topped with the lemon mixture.
6. You should cook the salmon for four to six minutes on each side, or until it achieves the amount of doneness that you choose.
7. To be served hot.

Tuscan Tuna and Zucchini Burgers

Ingredients:

- 2 cans tuna, drained
- 1 cup grated zucchini
- 1/4 cup chopped sun-dried tomatoes
- 2 tablespoons chopped fresh basil
- 2 tablespoons mayonnaise
- 1 tablespoon Dijon mustard
- 1/4 cup bread crumbs (or almond flour for a gluten-free option)
- Salt and pepper to taste
- Whole grain burger buns

Directions:

1. Tuna, shredded zucchini, sun-dried tomatoes, chopped basil, mayonnaise, Dijon mustard, bread crumbs, salt, and pepper should all be mixed together in a big basin.
2. Continue to stir until everything is well mixed.
3. Create burger patties out of the ingredients using your hands.
4. Prepare the grill or skillet by heating it over medium heat and greasing it generously with oil.
5. Cook the tuna and zucchini patties for 4-5 minutes each side, or until they have a golden brown color all the way through and are fully cooked.
6. You may serve the burgers on buns made from whole grains with whatever toppings you choose.

Stew with Cod

Ingredients:

- 1 pound cod fillets, cut into chunks
- 1 onion, diced
- 2 cloves garlic, minced
- 2 carrots, diced
- 2 celery stalks, diced
- 1 can diced tomatoes
- 4 cups vegetable broth
- 1 teaspoon dried thyme
- 1 teaspoon dried oregano
- Salt and pepper to taste
- Fresh parsley for garnish

Directions:

1. Start by warming some oil in a big saucepan set over medium heat.
2. To the pan, add the carrots, celery, carrots, and garlic. Sauté until softened.
3. You should now add the chopped tomatoes, the vegetable broth, the dried thyme, the dried oregano, as well as salt and pepper. Give everything a good stir.
4. Cook the stew for about 15 minutes after bringing it to a simmer.
5. After adding the cod fillets to the saucepan, give the mixture a little toss.
6. Keep the heat on low and simmer for an additional 10 to 12 minutes, or until the fish is completely cooked through and flakes easily.
7. The stew should be served steaming hot with a garnish of fresh chopped parsley.

Roasted Shrimp-Gnocchi

Ingredients:

- 1 pound shrimp, peeled and deveined
- 1 pound gnocchi
- 2 tablespoons olive oil
- 2 cloves garlic, minced
- 1 teaspoon dried Italian seasoning
- Salt and pepper to taste
- Fresh parsley for garnish

Directions:

1. Preheat the oven to 425°F (220°C).
2. In a large baking dish, toss the shrimp, gnocchi, olive oil, minced garlic, Italian seasoning, salt, and pepper until well combined.
3. Spread the mixture evenly in the baking dish.
4. Roast in the preheated oven for 15-20 minutes or until the shrimp is cooked through and the gnocchi is golden and crispy.
5. Garnish with fresh parsley and serve hot.

Sandwiches with Italian Tuna

Ingredients:

- 2 cans tuna, drained
- 1/4 cup mayonnaise
- 1 tablespoon Dijon mustard
- 2 tablespoons chopped red onion
- 2 tablespoons chopped celery
- 1 tablespoon chopped fresh parsley
- Salt and pepper to taste
- Whole grain bread
- Lettuce, tomato slices, and cucumber slices for topping

Directions:

1. Mix the tuna, mayonnaise, Dijon mustard, red onion, celery, parsley, salt, and pepper in a bowl until everything is well distributed. Combine thoroughly.
2. On pieces of whole grain bread, spread the tuna mixture using a spreader.
3. Add some lettuce on the top, along with tomato and cucumber slices.
4. To finish the sandwich, finish it off with another piece of bread on top.
5. The sandwich should be cut in half before being served.

Dill Salmon Salad Wraps

Ingredients:

- 1 pound cooked salmon, flaked
- 1/4 cup Greek yogurt
- 1 tablespoon lemon juice
- 2 tablespoons chopped fresh dill
- 1/4 cup diced cucumber
- Salt and pepper to taste
- Whole grain tortillas
- Spinach leaves for filling

Directions:

1. Mix together the flakes salmon, Greek yogurt, lemon juice, chopped dill, sliced cucumber, and seasonings with salt and pepper in a bowl. Combine thoroughly.
2. Place a layer of spinach leaves in the middle of a whole grain tortilla that has been laid out flat.
3. Place some of the smoked salmon salad on a tortilla.
4. To make a wrap using the tortilla, roll it up securely.
5. Proceed with the other components in the same manner.
6. If you so want, cut the wraps in half before serving.

White Clam Pizza Pie

Ingredients:

- 1 prepared pizza dough
- 1/2 cup marinara sauce
- 1 cup shredded mozzarella cheese
- 1 can chopped clams, drained
- 2 cloves garlic, minced
- 2 tablespoons chopped fresh parsley
- Red pepper flakes (optional)

Directions:

1. Prepare the pizza dough according to the instructions on the box, then preheat the oven to the recommended temperature.
2. The pizza dough should be rolled out and then placed on a baking pan.
3. Marinara sauce should be spread over the dough in a uniform layer.
4. Over the top of the sauce, sprinkle some shredded mozzarella cheese.
5. Chopped clams, minced garlic, and chopped parsley should be sprinkled on top.
6. Bake in an oven that has been warmed according to the directions on the box or until the crust is brown and the cheese is melted and bubbling, whichever comes first.
7. After removing from the oven, if desired, you may sprinkle it with dried red pepper flakes.
8. Cut and serve while still hot.

Mushroom Stew Made with Cod

Ingredients:

- 1 pound cod fillets, cut into chunks
- 8 ounces mushrooms, sliced
- 1 onion, chopped
- 2 cloves garlic, minced
- 2 tablespoons olive oil
- 1 can diced tomatoes
- 1 cup vegetable broth
- 1 teaspoon dried thyme
- Salt and pepper to taste
- Fresh parsley for garnish

Directions:

2. Heat olive oil in a big saucepan or skillet over medium heat.
3. Add the garlic that has been minced and the chopped onion. Sauté until the onion turns transparent.
4. After adding the sliced mushrooms, continue to sauté them until they begin to become more tender.
5. Mix in the diced tomatoes, dry thyme, diced vegetable broth, salt, and pepper in a mixing bowl.
6. Cook the mixture for around ten minutes after bringing it to a simmer.
7. Cod fillets should be added to the stew in a gentle manner.
8. Cover and continue simmering for eight to ten minutes, or until the fish is fully cooked and readily flakes apart.
9. Serve the stew piping hot, topped with chopped fresh parsley, and enjoy.

Baked Lemon Herb Chicken

Ingredients:

- 4 boneless, skinless chicken breasts
- 2 tablespoons olive oil
- Juice of 1 lemon
- 2 cloves garlic, minced
- 1 teaspoon dried thyme
- Salt and pepper to taste

Directions:

1. Set the temperature in the oven to 375 degrees Fahrenheit (190 degrees Celsius).
2. The chicken breasts should be placed in a baking dish.
3. Olive oil, lemon juice, minced garlic, dried thyme, ground pepper, and salt should be mixed together in a small bowl using a whisk.
4. After pouring the sauce over the chicken, make sure it coats the chicken completely.
5. Bake the chicken in an oven that has been warmed for 25 to 30 minutes, or until it is completely cooked through and the middle is no longer pink.
6. To be served hot.

Grilled Chicken with Mango Salsa

Ingredients:

- 4 boneless, skinless chicken breasts
- 1 ripe mango, diced
- 1/2 red bell pepper, diced
- 1/4 red onion, finely chopped
- Juice of 1 lime
- 2 tablespoons chopped fresh cilantro
- Salt and pepper to taste

Directions:

1. Prepare the grill by heating it to a medium-high temperature.
2. Add salt and pepper to the chicken breasts before cooking them.

3. Grill the chicken for six to eight minutes each side, or until the internal temperature reaches 165 degrees Fahrenheit (74 degrees Celsius), whichever comes first.
4. In the meanwhile, mix the diced mango, red bell pepper, and red onion with the lime juice, chopped cilantro, and the seasonings of your choice in a dish. To create the salsa, give everything a good stir.
5. Take the chicken off the grill and let it sit for a few minutes to allow the juices redistribute.
6. Mango salsa should be spread over each chicken breast before being served.

Honey Mustard Baked Chicken Thighs

Ingredients:

- 4 chicken thighs, bone-in and skin-on
- 2 tablespoons Dijon mustard
- 1 tablespoon honey
- 1 tablespoon olive oil
- 2 cloves garlic, minced
- 1 teaspoon dried thyme
- Salt and pepper to taste

Directions:

1. Put the oven on to a temperature of 425 degrees Fahrenheit (220 degrees Celsius).
2. Dijon mustard, honey, olive oil, chopped garlic, dried thyme, salt, and pepper should be mixed together in a small bowl using a whisk.
3. The chicken thighs should be placed in a baking dish.
4. Coat the chicken completely with the honey mustard mixture by brushing it on both sides.
5. Bake the chicken in an oven that has been warmed for 25 to 30 minutes, or until the chicken is fully cooked and the skin has become crispy.
6. When heated, serve

Lemon Herb Roasted Chicken

Ingredients:

- 1 whole chicken
- 2 lemons, sliced
- 4 cloves garlic, minced
- 2 tablespoons chopped fresh rosemary
- 2 tablespoons chopped fresh thyme
- 2 tablespoons olive oil
- Salt and pepper to taste

Directions:

1. Preheat the oven to 425°F (220°C).
2. Place the whole chicken in a roasting pan.
3. In a small bowl, mix together minced garlic, chopped rosemary, chopped thyme, olive oil, salt, and pepper.
4. Rub the mixture all over the chicken, including under the skin.
5. Stuff the cavity of the chicken with lemon slices.
6. Roast the chicken in the preheated oven for 1 hour and 15 minutes, or until the internal temperature reaches 165°F (74°C) and the skin is golden and crispy.
7. Let the chicken rest for a few minutes before carving. Serve hot.

Teriyaki Chicken Stir-Fry

Ingredients:

- 1 pound boneless, skinless chicken breast, cut into strips
- 1/4 cup low-sodium soy sauce
- 2 tablespoons honey
- 2 tablespoons rice vinegar
- 1 tablespoon sesame oil
- 2 cloves garlic, minced
- 1 tablespoon grated fresh ginger
- 1 cup broccoli florets
- 1 bell pepper, sliced
- 1 carrot, julienned
- 1/2 cup snow peas
- 1/2 cup sliced mushrooms
- 2 green onions, sliced
- 2 tablespoons cornstarch (optional, for thickening)
- Cooked brown rice for serving

Directions:

1. Combine the soy sauce, honey, rice vinegar, sesame oil, chopped garlic, and grated ginger in a small bowl and mix all of the ingredients together. Set aside.
2. In a big skillet or wok, bring one tablespoon of oil up to temperature over medium-high heat.
3. After adding the chicken strips to the pan, continue to cook them until they are browned on both sides and no longer pink in the center. Remove from the skillet and put aside.
4. Place the broccoli, bell pepper, carrot, snow peas, mushrooms, and cut green onions in the same pan. Stir-fry the veggies for around four to five minutes, or until they reach the desired crisp-tender consistency.
5. Place the cooked chicken back into the pan, then pour the teriyaki sauce over the chicken and the rest of the ingredients. Mix everything together to provide a uniform coating.
6. If you want the sauce to be thicker, you may form a slurry by combining one tablespoon of water with a tablespoon of cornstarch, and then add it to the pan. Continue to cook for one minute longer.
7. Cook some brown rice and serve it on the side with the teriyaki chicken stir-fry.

Greek Chicken Skewers

Ingredients:

- 1 pound boneless, skinless chicken breasts, cut into cubes
- 1/4 cup olive oil
- 2 tablespoons lemon juice
- 2 cloves garlic, minced
- 1 teaspoon dried oregano
- 1/2 teaspoon dried thyme
- Salt and pepper to taste
- Cherry tomatoes
- Red onion, cut into chunks
- Bell peppers, cut into chunks

Directions:

1. Olive oil, lemon juice, minced garlic, dried oregano, dried thyme, salt, and pepper are mixed together in a bowl using a whisk before being added to the bowl.
2. To the bowl, add the chicken cubes, and then toss them around so that they are coated in the marinade. Allow it to sit in the marinade for at least half an hour.
3. Prepare the barbecue or grill pan by heating it to a medium-high temperature.
4. Skewer some chicken that has been marinated, along with cherry tomatoes, bits of red onion, and chunks of bell pepper.
5. Cook the skewers over a grill for ten to twelve minutes, flipping them every so often, until the chicken is fully cooked and has a charred appearance.
6. Serve the Greek chicken skewers while they are still very hot.

Thai Basil Chicken

Ingredients:

- 1 pound boneless, skinless chicken thighs, sliced
- 2 tablespoons soy sauce
- 1 tablespoon fish sauce
- 1 tablespoon oyster sauce
- 1 tablespoon hoisin sauce
- 2 teaspoons brown sugar
- 2 tablespoons vegetable oil
- 4 cloves garlic, minced
- 1 red chili pepper, sliced
- 1 cup fresh basil leaves
- Lime wedges for serving

Directions:

1. Combine the soy sauce, fish sauce, oyster sauce, hoisin sauce, and brown sugar in a small bowl and mix together until smooth. Set aside.
2. Prepare the stir-fry in a large pan or wok by heating the vegetable oil over medium-high heat.
3. Garlic that has been minced and sliced chili pepper should be added to the pan. Cook in a wok for one minute.
4. After adding the chicken pieces to the pan, continue to cook them until they are browned and cooked all the way through.
5. After pouring the sauce mixture over the chicken, toss it to ensure that it is uniformly distributed.
6. The fresh basil leaves should be added to the pan, and the stir-frying should continue for one more minute or until the basil has wilted.
7. Take the chicken dish made with Thai basil off the fire and serve it with lime wedges.

Lemon Herb Turkey Cutlets

Ingredients:

- 1 pound turkey cutlets
- 2 tablespoons olive oil
- Juice of 1 lemon
- 2 cloves garlic, minced
- 1 teaspoon dried rosemary
- 1 teaspoon dried thyme
- Salt and pepper to taste

Directions:

1. Turn the temperature on the oven to 375 degrees Fahrenheit (190 degrees Celsius).
2. The turkey cutlets should be placed in a baking dish.
3. Olive oil, lemon juice, minced garlic, dried rosemary, dried thyme, salt, and pepper should be mixed together in a small bowl using a whisking motion.
4. When you pour the mixture over the turkey cutlets, you want to make sure that they are covered equally.
5. Bake the turkey in an oven that has been warmed for 15 to 20 minutes, or until it is completely cooked through and the middle is no longer pink.
6. To be served hot.

Coconut Curry Chicken

Ingredients:

- 1 pound boneless, skinless chicken breasts, cut into cubes
- 2 tablespoons curry powder
- 1 can coconut milk
- 1 onion, chopped
- 2 cloves garlic, minced
- 1 tablespoon grated fresh ginger
- 1 bell pepper, sliced
- 1 cup sliced carrots
- 1 cup broccoli florets
- 1 tablespoon olive oil
- Salt and pepper to taste
- Fresh cilantro for garnish

Directions:

1. Olive oil should be heated in either a big pan or a wok over medium-high heat.
2. In a pan, add the garlic that has been minced along with the chopped onion. Keep cooking the onion until it becomes a transparent white.
3. Cook the chicken cubes in the skillet until they are browned on both sides before adding them.
4. The chicken should be coated uniformly with curry powder, which should be sprinkled over it.
5. Coconut milk and grated ginger should be added at this point. Combine everything by giving it a thorough stir.
6. The bell pepper, carrots, and broccoli florets should be added to the pan after they have been cut. Add little salt and pepper before serving.
7. Cover the pan, reduce the heat to medium-low, and let it simmer for about 15 minutes, or until the chicken is fully cooked through and the veggies are soft.
8. Try it out, then make any necessary adjustments to the seasoning.
9. Serve the coconut curry chicken over cooked rice and accompany it with naan bread. Garnish with fresh cilantro before serving.

Pesto Grilled Chicken

Ingredients:

- 4 boneless, skinless chicken breasts
- 1/2 cup basil pesto
- 2 tablespoons olive oil
- Juice of 1 lemon
- Salt and pepper to taste

Directions:

1. Prepare the grill by heating it to a medium-high temperature.
2. Add salt and pepper to the chicken breasts before cooking them.
3. Combine the pesto made with the basil, olive oil, and lemon juice in a small bowl.
4. Coat the chicken breasts with the pesto mixture using a brush, being sure to cover all sides.
5. Grill the chicken for six to eight minutes each side, or until the internal temperature reaches 165 degrees Fahrenheit (74 degrees Celsius), whichever comes first.
6. After removing it from the grill, let it sit for a few minutes to cool off before serving.
7. Prepare the pesto grilled chicken and serve it with the sides of your choice.

Baked Herb and Parmesan Chicken Tenders:

Ingredients:

- 1 pound chicken tenders
- 1 cup breadcrumbs
- 1/2 cup grated Parmesan cheese
- 1 teaspoon dried basil
- 1 teaspoon dried oregano
- 1/2 teaspoon garlic powder
- 1/2 teaspoon paprika
- Salt and pepper to taste
- 2 eggs, beaten

Directions:

1. Prepare a baking sheet by lining it with parchment paper and preheating the oven to 400 degrees Fahrenheit (200 degrees Celsius).
2. Mix breadcrumbs, grated Parmesan cheese, dried basil, dried oregano, garlic powder, paprika, salt, and pepper in a basin that is not too deep.
3. After each chicken tender has been dipped in the beaten eggs, it should be coated in the breadcrumb mixture and gently pressed together to adhere.
4. Place the chicken tenders that have been coated on the baking sheet that has been prepared.
5. Bake for 15–20 minutes in an oven that has been prepared, or until the coating is golden brown and crispy and the chicken is cooked all the way through.
6. The chicken tenders that have been roasted with herbs and Parmesan should be served with a side of marinara sauce or another dipping sauce of your choice.

Chicken and Vegetable Stir-Fry

Ingredients:

- 1 pound boneless, skinless chicken breasts, sliced
- 2 tablespoons soy sauce
- 1 tablespoon oyster sauce
- 1 tablespoon hoisin sauce
- 2 tablespoons vegetable oil
- 2 cloves garlic, minced
- 1 tablespoon grated fresh ginger
- 1 bell pepper, sliced
- 1 cup broccoli florets
- 1 cup sliced mushrooms
- 1/2 cup sliced carrots
- 1/2 cup snap peas
- Salt and pepper to taste
- Cooked rice for serving

Directions:

1. Combine the soy sauce, oyster sauce, and hoisin sauce in a small bowl and whisk until smooth. Set aside.
2. Prepare the stir-fry in a large pan or wok by heating the vegetable oil over medium-high heat.
3. The skillet now has garlic that has been minced and ginger that has been grated. Stir-fry for 1 minute until aromatic.
4. When the chicken has reached an internal temperature of 165 degrees and has a golden brown color, remove it from the pan.
5. In a pan over medium heat, combine the bell pepper, broccoli florets, sliced mushrooms, sliced carrots, and snap peas. Stir-fry the veggies for three to four minutes, or until they reach a crisp-tender consistency.
6. The chicken and veggies should be covered in the sauce combination that has been prepared. Mix everything together to provide a uniform coating.
7. Salt and pepper should be added according to your preference.
8. Continue to cook for one more minute, or until the sauce has reached the desired consistency.
9. Turn off the heat and serve the chicken and vegetable stir-fry on top of rice that has already been cooked.

Baked Panko-Crusted Chicken

Ingredients:

- 4 boneless, skinless chicken breasts
- 1 cup panko breadcrumbs
- 1/2 cup grated Parmesan cheese
- 1 teaspoon dried Italian seasoning
- 1/2 teaspoon garlic powder
- Salt and pepper to taste
- 2 eggs, beaten
- Cooking spray

Directions:

1. Prepare a baking sheet by lining it with parchment paper and preheating the oven to 400 degrees Fahrenheit (200 degrees Celsius).
2. Panko breadcrumbs, grated Parmesan cheese, dry Italian seasoning, garlic powder, salt, and pepper should be mixed together in a basin that is not too deep.
3. After each chicken breast has been dipped in the eggs that have been beaten, it should be coated in the breadcrumb mixture and lightly pressed to adhere.
4. Place the chicken breasts that have been seasoned on the baking sheet that has been prepared.
5. Spray some cooking spray on top of each chicken breast so that it is lightly coated.
6. Cook the chicken in an oven that has been warmed for 20 to 25 minutes, or until it is completely cooked through and the coating is golden brown and crispy.
7. After removing it from the oven, let it sit for a few minutes to cool down before serving.
8. You may serve the roasted chicken with the panko coating with any of your favorite side dishes.

Meat

Grilled Lemon Herb Chicken

Ingredients:

- 4 boneless, skinless chicken breasts
- Juice of 2 lemons
- 2 tablespoons olive oil
- 2 cloves garlic, minced
- 1 teaspoon dried rosemary
- 1 teaspoon dried thyme
- Salt and pepper to taste

Directions:

1. In Mix the lemon juice, olive oil, minced garlic, dried rosemary, dried thyme, salt, and pepper in a small bowl using a whisk.
2. After placing the chicken breasts in a dish with a shallow depth, pour the marinade over them so that it coats all sides of the chicken. Allow it to sit in the marinade for at least half an hour.
3. Prepare the grill by heating it to a medium-high temperature.
4. Cook the chicken breasts on the grill for six to eight minutes per side, or until the internal temperature reaches 165 degrees Fahrenheit (74 degrees Celsius).
5. Take them off the grill and give them a few minutes to rest before serving.

Baked Turkey Meatballs

Ingredients:

- 1 pound ground turkey
- 1/2 cup whole wheat breadcrumbs
- 1/4 cup grated Parmesan cheese
- 1/4 cup chopped fresh parsley
- 1 egg
- 2 cloves garlic, minced
- 1/2 teaspoon dried oregano
- 1/2 teaspoon dried basil
- Salt and pepper to taste
- Marinara sauce for serving

Directions:

1. Prepare a baking sheet by lining it with parchment paper and preheating the oven to 400 degrees Fahrenheit (200 degrees Celsius).
2. Mix ground turkey, breadcrumbs, grated Parmesan cheese, chopped parsley, an egg, minced garlic, dried oregano, dried basil, salt, and pepper together in a large bowl. Combine everything by thoroughly combining it.
3. Form the mixture into meatballs with a diameter of approximately 1 inch and place them on the baking sheet that has been prepared.
4. Bake the meatballs in an oven that has been preheated to 350 degrees for 15 to 20 minutes, or until they are browned and cooked through.
5. Marinara sauce and the side dishes of your choice can be served alongside the turkey meatballs.

Turkey Chili

Ingredients:

- 1 pound ground turkey
- 1 onion, chopped
- 2 cloves garlic, minced
- 1 bell pepper, chopped
- 1 can (15 ounces) kidney beans, rinsed and drained
- 1 can (15 ounces) black beans, rinsed and drained
- 1 can (14.5 ounces) diced tomatoes
- 1 can (8 ounces) tomato sauce
- 1 tablespoon chili powder
- 1 teaspoon cumin
- 1 teaspoon paprika
- Salt and pepper to taste
- Optional toppings: shredded cheese, chopped green onions, sour cream

Directions:

1. Olive oil should be heated over medium heat in a Dutch oven or other large pot.
2. To the pot, add chopped onion, garlic that has been minced, and chopped bell pepper. Sauté the vegetables until they reach the desired degree of tenderness.
3. After the ground turkey has been cooked and browned, remove it from the pot and break it up into smaller pieces.
4. Mix in the chili powder, cumin, paprika, and salt and pepper to taste after each addition. Toast the spices by continuing to cook for another minute.
5. In a large pot, combine the kidney beans, black beans, diced tomatoes, and tomato sauce. Stir to combine. Stir to combine.
6. Bring the mixture up to a simmer, after which cover the pot and reduce the heat to a low setting. Allow it to simmer for at least half an hour so that the flavors can combine and become more pronounced.
7. Try it out, and make any necessary adjustments to the seasoning.
8. To serve, ladle the hot turkey chili into bowls and top with the toppings of your choice.

Beef and Vegetable Stir-Fry

Ingredients:

- 1 pound beef sirloin, thinly sliced
- 2 tablespoons soy sauce
- 1 tablespoon oyster sauce
- 1 tablespoon hoisin sauce
- 1 tablespoon cornstarch
- 2 tablespoons vegetable oil
- 2 cloves garlic, minced
- 1 tablespoon grated fresh ginger
- 1 bell pepper, sliced
- 1 cup broccoli florets
- 1 cup sliced mushrooms
- 1/2 cup sliced carrots
- Salt and pepper to taste
- Cooked rice or noodles for serving

Directions:

1. Soy sauce, oyster sauce, hoisin sauce, and cornstarch should be mixed together in a small basin using a whisk. Set aside.
2. Prepare the stir-fry in a large pan or wok by heating the vegetable oil over medium-high heat.
3. The skillet now has garlic that has been minced and ginger that has been grated. Stir-fry for 1 minute until aromatic.
4. When the meat has reached the desired doneness, remove from the pan and set aside. Remove from the skillet and put aside.
5. Place the bell pepper, broccoli florets, sliced mushrooms, and carrots that have been cut into strips in the same pan. Stir-fry the veggies for three to four minutes, or until they reach a crisp-tender consistency.
6. Place the meat that has been cooked back into the pan, and then pour the sauce mixture over the steak and the rest of the ingredients. Mix well to provide a uniform coating.
7. Continue to cook for one more minute, or until the sauce has reached the desired consistency.
8. Salt and pepper may be added to taste as a seasoning.

9. Turn off the heat and serve the meat and vegetable stir-fry on rice or noodles that have been previously prepared.

Honey Mustard Glazed Ham

Ingredients:

- 1 fully cooked bone-in ham (about 8 pounds)
- 1/2 cup Dijon mustard
- 1/2 cup honey
- 2 tablespoons brown sugar
- 2 tablespoons apple cider vinegar
- 1 teaspoon ground cloves

Directions:

1. Put the oven on to a temperature of 325 degrees Fahrenheit (163 degrees Celsius).
2. Put the ham in a roasting pan that has a rack in it and make sure the cut side is facing down.
3. Dijon mustard, honey, brown sugar, apple cider vinegar, and powdered cloves should be mixed together in a small basin using a whisk.
4. Coat the ham well with the honey mustard glaze by applying it in thick layers and brushing it on from all sides.
5. Bake the ham with a loose covering of aluminum foil for 15 minutes per pound, or until it reaches an internal temperature of 140 degrees Fahrenheit (60 degrees Celsius).
6. During the last 15 minutes of baking, take off the foil to enable the glaze to brown and become caramelized.
7. After it has finished cooking, take the ham out of the oven and let it rest for at least ten to fifteen minutes before slicing it.
8. Ham with a honey mustard glaze may be served with any of your favorite side dishes.

Moroccan Spiced Lamb Chops

Ingredients:

- 8 lamb chops
- 2 tablespoons olive oil
- 2 teaspoons ground cumin
- 2 teaspoons ground coriander
- 1 teaspoon ground paprika
- 1/2 teaspoon ground cinnamon
- 1/2 teaspoon ground ginger
- Salt and pepper to taste
- Fresh cilantro for garnish

Directions:

1. Prepare the grill or a pan that may be used as a grill by heating it over medium-high heat.
2. Mix together ground ginger, ground cinnamon, ground coriander, ground cumin, and ground paprika in a small dish. Season with ground salt and ground pepper.
3. Olive oil should be used to coat the lamb chops, and then the spice mixture should be sprinkled over them and gently pressed to adhere.
4. In order to get a medium-rare doneness, the lamb chops should have an internal temperature of 145 degrees Fahrenheit (63 degrees Celsius) after being grilled for three to four minutes on each side.
5. Take them off the grill and let them a few minutes to rest before serving.
6. Serve the Moroccan-spiced lamb chops with the side dishes of your choice, and garnish with fresh cilantro before serving.

Korean-Style Beef Bulgogi

Ingredients:

- 1 pound beef sirloin, thinly sliced
- 1/4 cup soy sauce
- 2 tablespoons brown sugar
- 2 tablespoons sesame oil
- 2 cloves garlic, minced
- 1 tablespoon grated fresh ginger
- 1 tablespoon rice vinegar
- 2 green onions, chopped
- 1 tablespoon sesame seeds
- Cooked rice or lettuce leaves for serving

Directions:

1. Mix together the soy sauce, brown sugar, sesame oil, minced garlic, grated ginger, sliced green onions, and sesame seeds in a bowl using a whisk.
2. Add the beef slices to the marinade and allow them to marinate for at least 30 minutes; for an even deeper flavor, marinate the steak overnight in the refrigerator.
3. Prepare a grill pan or a big skillet by heating it over medium-high heat.
4. Cook the beef that has been marinated in batches for two to three minutes on each side, or until it is browned and cooked all the way through.
5. Take the steak out of the pan and continue the process with the remaining meat.
6. Bulgogi, a traditional dish from Korea, may be served piping hot over boiled rice or wrapped in lettuce leaves.

Snacks

Apple Slices with Almond Butter

Ingredients:

- 1 apple, sliced
- 2 tablespoons almond butter

Directions:

1. Cut the apple into thin rounds or wedges using a sharp knife.
2. Spread a thin layer of almond butter on both sides of each apple slice.
3. To enjoy this delicious and filling snack, arrange the apple slices in a pretty pattern on a platter.

Rice Cake with Avocado and Tomato:

Ingredients:

- 1 rice cake
- 1/4 avocado, sliced
- 1 small tomato, sliced
- Salt and pepper to taste

Directions:

1. Place a rice cake on a plate.
2. Top it with sliced avocado and tomato.
3. Season with salt and pepper.
4. Enjoy this crunchy and refreshing snack.

Homemade Trail Mix

Ingredients:

- 1/2 cup unsalted almonds
- 1/2 cup cashews
- 1/2 cup dried cranberries
- 1/4 cup dark chocolate chips
- 1/4 cup pumpkin seeds

Directions:

1. Put all of the ingredients in a bowl and give the mixture a good stir.
2. Transfer the trail mix to separate bags large enough for one serving each for convenient on-the-go munching.
3. This homemade trail mix has an adequate amount of all three essential nutrients: protein, healthy fats, and fiber.

Cucumber Slices with Cottage Cheese

Ingredients:

- 1 cucumber, sliced
- 1/2 cup cottage cheese
- Dill or other herbs for garnish (optional)

Directions:

1. Arrange the cucumber slices in a decorative pattern on the platter.
2. Place a glob of cottage cheese on top of each individual piece.

Baked Sweet Potato Chips

Ingredients:

- 2 medium sweet potatoes
- 2 tablespoons olive oil
- Salt and pepper to taste

Directions:

1. Prepare a baking sheet by lining it with parchment paper and heating the oven to 375 degrees Fahrenheit (190 degrees Celsius).
2. Use a mandoline slicer or a sharp knife to cut the sweet potatoes into circular slices of a very thin thickness.
3. Place the sweet potato slices in a bowl and add the olive oil, salt, and pepper. Toss until the pieces are uniformly coated.
4. Arrange the slices so that they are in a single layer on the baking sheet that has been prepared.
5. Bake for 15–20 minutes, or until the chips have achieved the desired crispiness and color.
6. Wait until they have cooled down before indulging in these flavorful and healthier alternatives to traditional potato chips.

Quinoa Salad Cups

Ingredients:

- 1 cup cooked quinoa
- 1 cup diced vegetables (such as cucumber, bell peppers, cherry tomatoes)
- 1/4 cup crumbled feta cheese
- 2 tablespoons chopped fresh herbs (such as parsley, mint, basil)
- Juice of 1 lemon
- Salt and pepper to taste
- Lettuce cups or endive leaves for serving

Directions:

1. Mix together in a bowl the quinoa that has been cooked, the vegetables that have been diced, the crumbled feta cheese, the fresh herbs that have been cut, the lemon juice, salt, and pepper. Combine thoroughly.
2. Place a scoop of the quinoa salad mixture into the center of each endive leaf or lettuce cup.
3. As a refreshing and wholesome option for a snack that's light but yet filling, try these individual quinoa salad cups.

Turkey Roll-Ups

Ingredients:

- Sliced turkey breast (about 4-6 slices)
- 2 tablespoons cream cheese
- 1/2 cucumber, cut into matchstick-sized strips
- Fresh basil leaves

Directions:

1. Arrange the turkey slices in a level layer on a surface that has been cleaned.
2. Each slice should have a very thin coating of cream cheese spread on it.
3. On top of the cream cheese, arrange the cucumber strips and fresh basil leaves in a decorative pattern.
4. If necessary, use toothpicks to hold the turkey slices in place after rolling them securely.
5. Cut the roll-ups into pieces that are suitable for snacking.

6. One option for a snack that is both high in protein and low in carbs is provided by these turkey roll-ups.

Spiced Roasted Chickpeas

Ingredients:

- 1 can (15 ounces) chickpeas, drained and rinsed
- 1 tablespoon olive oil
- 1 teaspoon ground cumin
- 1/2 teaspoon paprika
- 1/2 teaspoon garlic powder
- 1/4 teaspoon cayenne pepper (optional)
- Salt to taste

Directions:

1. Prepare a baking sheet by lining it with parchment paper and preheating the oven to 400 degrees Fahrenheit (200 degrees Celsius).
2. Using a paper towel, thoroughly pat the chickpeas until they are dry.
3. To ensure that the chickpeas are evenly covered with the spices and seasonings, mix them in a dish with some olive oil, ground cumin, paprika, garlic powder, and cayenne pepper (if using).
4. Place the chickpeas that have been seasoned in a single layer on the baking sheet that has been prepared.
5. Bake the chickpeas for 25 to 30 minutes, or until they reach the desired level of crispiness and color.
6. Before nibbling on these delicious roasted chickpeas that are filled with protein, give them some time to cool down.

Zucchini Pizza Bites

Ingredients:

- 2 medium zucchini, cut into rounds
- Tomato sauce
- Shredded mozzarella cheese
- Sliced cherry tomatoes
- Fresh basil leaves
- Olive oil
- Salt and pepper to taste

Directions:

1. Prepare a baking sheet by lining it with parchment paper and preheating the oven to 400 degrees Fahrenheit (200 degrees Celsius).
2. After placing the rounds of zucchini on the baking sheet, brush them with olive oil.
3. On each round of zucchini, evenly spread a little quantity of tomato sauce.
4. On top of the sauce, sprinkle some grated or shredded mozzarella cheese.
5. On each of the rounds, place a tomato cherry that has been cut and seasoned with salt and pepper.
6. Bake the cheese for 12 to 15 minutes, or until it is melted and bubbling, whichever comes first.
7. Serve as a more nutritious alternative to pizza, then garnish with fresh basil leaves before serving.

Turkey and Veggie Pinwheels

Ingredients:

- Whole-grain tortillas
- Sliced turkey breast
- Sliced avocado
- Shredded carrots
- Baby spinach leaves
- Hummus or mustard for spreading

Directions:

1. Spread a small coating of hummus or mustard on the top of a tortilla that has been laid out flat.
2. On top of it, arrange thinly sliced turkey breast, baby spinach leaves, avocado slices, and carrots that have been shredded.
3. To make a log-like form with the tortilla, roll it up firmly.
4. Proceed with the rest of the tortillas and the ingredients in the same manner.
5. Cut the rolls into pinwheels that are suitable for nibbling.
6. Pinwheels made of turkey and vegetables provide a healthy meal that can easily be taken on the go.

Baked Egg Cups

Ingredients:

- Eggs
- Chopped vegetables (such as bell peppers, spinach, mushrooms)
- Diced cooked chicken or turkey (optional)
- Shredded cheese
- Salt and pepper to taste

Directions:

1. Put the muffin tray in the oven and preheat it to 375 degrees Fahrenheit (190 degrees Celsius).
2. Add a combination of chopped veggies, diced cooked chicken or turkey (if using), and a sprinkling of shredded cheese to each muffin cup. If using, you may also use turkey.
3. Each muffin cup should have an egg cracked into it.
4. Add little salt and pepper before serving.
5. Bake for 15-18 minutes or until the eggs are set.
6. Before removing the egg cups from the muffin pan, you should give them some time to cool down somewhat.
7. As a fast and satiating snack option, you may serve these baked egg cups filled with protein.

Veggie

Zucchini Noodles with Pesto

Ingredients:

- 2 medium zucchini
- 1/2 cup fresh basil leaves
- 1/4 cup pine nuts
- 2 cloves garlic
- 1/4 cup grated Parmesan cheese
- 1/4 cup olive oil
- Salt and pepper to taste
- Cherry tomatoes for garnish

Directions:

1. Make zucchini "noodles" by passing the zucchini through a spiralizer or a vegetable peeler.
2. Fresh basil leaves, pine nuts, garlic, Parmesan cheese, olive oil, and seasonings such as salt and pepper should be combined in a food processor. Combine until there are no lumps.
3. To ensure that the zucchini noodles are evenly covered with the pesto sauce, give them a good toss.

4. If you want, you may top the dish with cherry tomatoes and more grated Parmesan cheese.
5. We hope you like this recipe of tasty zucchini noodles that is light and refreshing.

Roasted Vegetable Medley

Ingredients:

- Assorted vegetables (such as carrots, broccoli, cauliflower, bell peppers, zucchini)
- 2 tablespoons olive oil
- 1 teaspoon dried herbs (such as thyme, rosemary, or Italian seasoning)
- Salt and pepper to taste

Directions:

1. Prepare a baking sheet by lining it with parchment paper and preheating the oven to 425 degrees Fahrenheit (220 degrees Celsius).
2. To make the veggies easier to eat, chop them into little pieces.
3. To ensure that the veggies are evenly covered with the olive oil, dried herbs, salt, and pepper, toss them in a dish.
4. The veggies should be spread out in a single layer on the baking sheet that has been prepared.
5. Roast the veggies for 25 to 30 minutes, or until they reach the desired level of tenderness and a light golden brown color.
6. You can add this vibrant and nutrient-dense side dish to salads and grain bowls, or serve it on its own.

Spinach and Mushroom Stuffed Portobello Mushrooms:

Ingredients:

- 4 large portobello mushrooms
- 2 cups fresh spinach leaves
- 1 cup diced mushrooms
- 1/4 cup diced onion
- 2 cloves garlic, minced
- 1/4 cup grated Parmesan cheese
- 2 tablespoons breadcrumbs (optional)
- 2 tablespoons olive oil
- Salt and pepper to taste

Directions:

1. Prepare a baking sheet by lining it with parchment paper and heating the oven to 375 degrees Fahrenheit (190 degrees Celsius).
2. Portobello mushroom stems should be removed, and the caps should be well cleaned.
3. In a pan, heat olive oil over medium heat. Mix in some chopped garlic, onion, and mushrooms.
4. Continue cooking over medium heat until the mushrooms are fork tender and all of the liquid has been absorbed.
5. When the fresh spinach leaves have wilted, remove them from the heat and set aside. Take the pan off the heat.
6. Mix the sautéed mushroom and spinach combination with grated Parmesan cheese and breadcrumbs, if using any of those ingredients, in a basin designated for mixing. Add little salt and pepper before serving.
7. Place a good amount of the mixture into the caps of the portobello mushrooms using a spoon.
8. Put the filled mushrooms on the baking sheet that has been prepared, and bake them for 15 to 20 minutes, or until the mushrooms are soft and the filling is brown.
9. Prepare as a savory and filling main course option for vegetarians.

Cauliflower Fried Rice

Ingredients:

- 1 small head cauliflower, grated or processed into rice-like texture
- 1 cup mixed vegetables (such as peas, carrots, corn)
- 1/2 cup diced bell peppers
- 1/2 cup diced onion
- 2 cloves garlic, minced
- 2 tablespoons low-sodium soy sauce
- 1 tablespoon sesame oil
- 2 green onions, sliced
- 2 eggs, beaten (optional)
- Salt and pepper to taste

Directions:

1. Warm the sesame oil in a large saucepan or wok set over a moderate heat. To this, add minced garlic, onion, and peppers of various colors. Sauté until the veggies are soft.
2. Place the whisked eggs on the other side of the skillet from the veggies, and then push the vegetables to one side of the pan. Eggs should be scrambled until they are done.
3. In a pan, combine the cauliflower that has been grated, the mixed veggies, the low-sodium soy sauce, the salt, and the pepper. Stir-fry for three to five minutes, or until the cauliflower is fork-tender and the flavors have been well incorporated.
4. After removing it from the fire, garnish it with chopped green onions.
5. As a healthy and low-carb alternative to regular fried rice, serve the cauliflower fried rice instead.

Lentil and Vegetable Curry

Ingredients:

- 1 cup dried lentils, rinsed
- 1 onion, diced
- 2 cloves garlic, minced
- 1 tablespoon curry powder
- 1 teaspoon ground cumin
- 1 teaspoon ground turmeric
- 1/2 teaspoon ground ginger
- 1 can (14 ounces) diced tomatoes
- 1 cup vegetable broth
- 2 cups chopped vegetables (such as carrots, bell peppers, zucchini)
- 1 cup coconut milk
- 2 tablespoons olive oil
- Salt and pepper to taste
- Fresh cilantro for garnish

Directions:

1. Olive oil should be heated in a large saucepan over medium heat. To this, add minced garlic and chopped onion. Sauté until the onion is transparent.
2. Curry powder, cumin, turmeric, and ginger should be added to the saucepan. Stir and continue cooking for one to two minutes, or until the aroma is released.
3. In a large saucepan, combine lentils that have been washed, diced tomatoes along with their juice, vegetable broth, veggies that have been chopped, coconut milk, salt, and pepper. Combine everything by giving it a thorough stir.
4. Bring the mixture to a boil, then immediately decrease the heat and allow it simmer for 20 to 25 minutes, or until the lentils and veggies are cooked and the flavors have merged together.
5. If necessary, make adjustments to the seasoning.
6. Rice that has been cooked and naan bread may be served with the lentil and veggie stew. Add some fresh cilantro as a garnish.

Roasted Brussels Sprouts with Balsamic Glaze:

Ingredients:

- 1 pound Brussels sprouts, trimmed and halved
- 2 tablespoons olive oil
- 2 tablespoons balsamic vinegar
- 1 tablespoon honey or maple syrup
- Salt and pepper to taste

Directions:

1. Prepare a baking sheet by lining it with parchment paper and preheating the oven to 425 degrees Fahrenheit (220 degrees Celsius).
2. To ensure that the Brussels sprouts are evenly covered with the olive oil, salt, and pepper, toss them in a basin.
3. Place the Brussels sprouts in a single layer on the baking sheet that has been prepared for them.
4. Roast the Brussels sprouts in the oven for 20 to 25 minutes, or until they have a caramelized appearance and are soft, tossing once halfway through the cooking time.
5. Warm the honey or maple syrup together with the balsamic vinegar in a small saucepan over low heat until the mixture begins to thicken into the consistency of a glaze.
6. After the Brussels sprouts have finished roasting, drizzle them with the balsamic glaze and toss them lightly to coat.
7. Serve as an appetizing and wholesome accompaniment to a meal.

Side dishes

Garlic Roasted Asparagus

Ingredients:

- 1 bunch asparagus, trimmed
- 2 tablespoons olive oil
- 2 cloves garlic, minced
- Salt and pepper to taste
- Lemon wedges for serving (optional)

Directions:

1. Prepare a baking sheet by lining it with parchment paper and preheating the oven to 425 degrees Fahrenheit (220 degrees Celsius).
2. Arrange the trimmed asparagus in a single layer on the baking sheet that has been previously prepared.
3. The asparagus should be seasoned with minced garlic, salt, and pepper before being drizzled with olive oil. To get an equal coating, toss the asparagus.
4. Roast the asparagus in the oven for 10 to 15 minutes, or until it is cooked through but still has some crunch.

5. Before serving, if desired, drizzle the roasted asparagus with fresh lemon juice that has been squeezed over it.

Quinoa and Vegetable Salad

Ingredients:

- 1 cup cooked quinoa
- 1 cup mixed vegetables (such as diced cucumber, cherry tomatoes, bell peppers)
- 1/4 cup chopped fresh herbs (such as parsley, cilantro, or basil)
- 2 tablespoons lemon juice
- 2 tablespoons olive oil
- Salt and pepper to taste

Directions:

1. Mix quinoa that has been cooked, a variety of veggies, and fresh herbs that have been chopped together in a bowl.
2. To prepare the dressing, place the lemon juice, olive oil, salt, and pepper in a small container and mix well with a whisk.
3. The quinoa and vegetable combination should be poured with the dressing on top. Mix everything together by giving it a good toss.
4. If necessary, make adjustments to the seasoning.
5. You may serve the salad made with quinoa and vegetables refrigerated or at room temperature.

Grilled Vegetable Skewers

Ingredients:

- Assorted vegetables (such as bell peppers, zucchini, cherry tomatoes, red onions, mushrooms)
- Olive oil for brushing
- Salt and pepper to taste
- Fresh herbs (such as rosemary or thyme) for garnish

Directions:

1. Prepare the grill for cooking over a medium heat.
2. To make the veggies easier to eat, cut them into smaller pieces.
3. Skewer the veggies, switching the types as you go, on the wooden skewers.
4. Olive oil should be brushed on the veggie skewers, and then they should be seasoned with salt and pepper.
5. After the grill has been prepared, place the skewers on the grill and cook for 10 to 15 minutes, turning them regularly, until the veggies are charred and soft.
6. After removing the skewers from the grill, prepare the dish by topping them with a variety of fresh herbs.

Roasted Garlic Mashed Cauliflower

Ingredients:

- 1 head cauliflower, cut into florets
- 4 cloves garlic
- 2 tablespoons olive oil
- 1/4 cup unsweetened almond milk (or any milk of choice)
- Salt and pepper to taste
- Chopped chives or green onions for garnish

Directions:

1. Turn the temperature on the oven to 400 degrees Fahrenheit (200 degrees Celsius).
2. On a baking sheet, spread out the cauliflower florets and garlic cloves that are still intact. Salt and pepper to taste, then drizzle with olive oil. Toss in order to coat.
3. Roast the cauliflower in the oven for about 25 to 30 minutes, or until it is soft and golden brown.
4. Move the roasted cauliflower and garlic to the processing bowl of a food processor or blender. Add almond milk, salt, and pepper.
5. Blend until completely smooth and creamy, adjusting the consistency as necessary by adding more almond milk.
6. After you have mashed the cauliflower, place it in a serving dish and top it with some chopped chives or green onions.

Balsamic Roasted Brussels Sprouts with Cranberries:

Ingredients:

- 1 pound Brussels sprouts, trimmed and halved
- 2 tablespoons balsamic vinegar
- 1 tablespoon olive oil
- 1 tablespoon honey or maple syrup
- 1/2 cup dried cranberries
- Salt and pepper to taste
- Chopped walnuts for garnish (optional)

Directions:

1. Prepare a baking sheet by lining it with parchment paper and preheating the oven to 400 degrees Fahrenheit (200 degrees Celsius).
2. Mix together the balsamic vinegar, olive oil, honey or maple syrup, and the seasonings of your choice in a large bowl.
3. After cutting the Brussels sprouts in half, add them to the bowl and toss them so that they are equally coated with the mixture.
4. Transfer the Brussels sprouts to the baking sheet that has been prepared, and arrange them so that they are in a single layer.
5. Roast the Brussels sprouts in the oven for 20 to 25 minutes, or until they have a caramelized appearance and are soft, tossing once halfway through the cooking time.
6. After roasting the Brussels sprouts, remove them from the oven and top them with dried cranberries. Combine everything by gently tossing it.
7. Place in a plate intended for serving, and top with chopped walnuts, if you so want.

Conclusion

In conclusion, sustaining a diet that is both balanced and nutritious requires the consumption of health meals on a consistent basis. They provide the body with the essential nutrients, vitamins, and minerals that are required for it to operate at its highest potential. Your general health and ability to maintain a healthy weight may be improved and supported by ensuring that the foods you eat at each meal include a range of whole grains, legumes, lean meats, vegetables, and fruits.

Meals that are considered healthy often have a limited amount of processed foods, added sugars, and saturated fats. As a result, they are excellent for maintaining healthy blood sugar levels, cardiovascular health, and weight. You'll have more say over the kind and amount of food you eat if you cook your own meals at home using fresh, healthful foods. This gives you more autonomy over your diet.

When it comes to preparing healthy meals, it is essential to take into account the specific requirements and tastes of each person. Whether you adhere to a certain diet, such as a vegetarian or gluten-free one, or have specific nutritional objectives, there are a great number of recipes and alternatives available that may accommodate a wide variety of preferences and needs.

A healthy connection with food may also be supported by practicing portion management and paying attention to the signs provided by the body about when it is hungry and when it has had enough to eat. If you want to have continuous energy throughout the day, it is advised that you have a balance of macronutrients (carbohydrates, proteins, and healthy fats) in your meals.

Keep in mind that a healthy diet is not about restriction but rather about finding a sustainable method that feeds your body while still allowing for occasional pleasures. The key to a healthy diet is to discover such an approach. Incorporating regular physical exercise, maintaining enough hydration, and placing a high priority on self-care are also critical components of a holistic approach to achieving and maintaining optimal health and well-being.

In general, scrumptious, entertaining, and filling meals may be prepared using healthy ingredients. You may prepare meals that enhance energy and contribute to long-term health by being careful of the decisions you make, the materials you use, and the cooking techniques you use.

COOKING CONVERSION CHART

WEIGHT

IMPERIAL	METRIC
1/2 oz	15 g
1 oz	29 g
2 oz	57 g
3 oz	85 g
4 oz	113 g
5 oz	141 g
6 oz	170 g
8 oz	227 g
10 oz	283 g
12 oz	340 g
13 oz	369 g
14 oz	397 g
15 oz	425 g
1 lb	453 g

MEASUREMENT

CUP	ONCES	MILLILITERS	TABLESPOONS
8 cup	64 oz	1895 ml	128
6 cup	48 oz	1420 ml	96
5 cup	40 oz	1180 ml	80
4 cup	32 oz	960 ml	64
2 cup	16 oz	480 ml	32
1 cup	8 oz	240 ml	16
3/4 cup	6 oz	177 ml	12
2/3 cup	5 oz	158 ml	11
1/2 cup	4 oz	118 ml	8
3/8 cup	3 oz	90 ml	6
1/3 cup	2.5 oz	79 ml	5.5
1/4 cup	2 oz	59 ml	4
1/8 cup	1 oz	30 ml	3
1/16 cup	1/2 oz	15 ml	1

TEMPERATURE

FAHRENHEIT	CELSIUS
100 ºF	37 ºC
150 ºF	65 ºC
200 ºF	93 ºC
250 ºF	121 ºC
300 ºF	150 ºC
325 ºF	160 ºC
350 ºF	180 ºC
375 ºF	190 ºC
400 ºF	200 ºC
425 ºF	220 ºC
450 ºF	230 ºC
500 ºF	260 ºC
525 ºF	274 ºC
550 ºF	288 ºC

Made in the USA
Las Vegas, NV
03 September 2023

76978550R00063